<u>I'M ON VACATION:</u>
The Aftershow
Special

The Follow-up
Segment of
SCANDAL'S
"Who Wants To Be A
President
(By Marrying A
Bioterrorist)?"
episode in
The Dear
Recruiter/FBI/DoHS
series showcase
@
<u>TinyURL/DearHomela</u>
<u>ndSecurity</u>
on Amazon.com

CONTENTS:

1. A Few of My Journal Entries & Actual Real Letters To The FBI & Homeland Security

2. Excerpt From "The Party: Welcome To Oz"

3. The Baker Act Song

4. I'm On Vacation: The Aftershow Special-- The Follow-Up To The "Who Wants To Be A President By Marrying A Bioterrorist?" Segment of The "Dear Recruiter: SCANDAL!" Collection of Shorts

Dear Everybody:

Especially Homeland Security & The FBI
And The Office of The President of The United States of America

No one will allow any harm or health concern to come to my actual legitimate non-impersonated non-clone mother, Trudy Perkins, who raised me as a child. I see now that the reason why the version of her who lives with me can't sing like her is that she's the clone of my mom, whereas my real mom can sing circles around her clone-- because she knows how to use her vocal instrument. I just don't know where my real mom is. My mother's clone will be admitted to a mental hospital-- unharmed. I will update my published books accordingly.

Nobody dies because of something I said-- but all threats, active violators, and mortal enemies of me and mine (who survive The Reckoning) will be cryogenics chambered in outer space now-- for 700 years. #ForeverSleep

But know this:

YOU CAN'T TERRORIZE & ASSAULT ME
INTO GIVING YOU WHAT YOU WANT.

And to all you rapey nuts out there who think you're "just doing your job" or who think you're "helping me by hurting me" (you know who you are)-- it's long past time for your mucked up spy culture to learn that NO doesn't mean YES, NO doesn't mean MAYBE and NO sure as hell doesn't mean HELL YEAH-- as many of *you seemed to think you were hearing whenever you heard me SCREAMING MY F***ING LUNGS OFF AT YOU.*

<u>*NO - means - NO!*</u>

<u>*It aint that complicated.*</u>

<u>*But it seems you've all made it a very hard lesson to learn.*</u>

<u>*Well class,*</u>

<u>*Let's begin with--*</u>

<u>*The 50 Shades of Rape:*</u>

1st Degree Rape AKA Traditional Rape =
Forcing your body into another body

2nd Degree Rape AKA Facilitation Rape =
Facilitating 1st Degree Rape (e.g. Pimping and Sex Slave Trafficking)

3rd Degree Rape AKA Bioterrorism / Techno Rape =
Forcing your physical will on or into another body remotely (like pushing a button on a remote control device which then sends a signal that inflicts pain, torture, abuse, agony, anguish, suffering, or even just mild discomfort (in other words: UNINVITED PENETRATION, UNWANTED CONTACT OR "BAD TOUCH") onto another being without their knowledge AND consent). ~ I also call this form of rape/bioterrorism via an instrument of power (e.g. wand/phone), "The Cruciatus Curse"

(from The Harry Potter series) BECAUSE IT FEELS EXACTLY LIKE IT:

"The Cruciatus Curse[1] (Crucio),[1] also known as the Torture Curse,[5] was a tool of the Dark Arts and one of the three Unforgivable Curses. It was one of the most powerful and sinister spells known to Wizardkind. When cast successfully the curse inflicted intense, excruciating pain on the victim. The penalty for the use of this curse on another human being was a life sentence in Azkaban, unless there was sufficient enough evidence that the caster did so under the influence of the Imperius Curse.[1] Effect: Excruciating pain, insanity if victim is subjected for too long." Quote Source: https://harrypotter.fandom.com/wiki/Cruciatus_Curse

4th Degree Rape AKA Brain Rape = Forcing your consciousness into another being's headspace without their knowledge or consent-- or overriding their consciousness without their knowledge or consent, even if you got their consent to avatar them through uploading your consciousness into their headspace without overriding their consciousness. #InvasionOfTheBodySnatchers AKA #PodPeople ~ or the chemically induced Oculus equivalent of mind-controlling others = #NightOfTheLivingDead AKA #ZombiePeople ~ I also call this form of rape via an instrument of power (e.g. wand/phone), "The Imperious Curse" (from the Harry Potter series) BECAUSE IT SOUNDS EXACTLY LIKE IT:

"The Imperius Curse is one of the three Unforgivable Curses. When cast successfully, it places the victim completely under the caster's control, though a person with exceptional strength of will is capable of resisting it. If the Imperius Curse is performed poorly, then the victim would have their mind addled, an example being Muggle Junior Minister Herbert Chorley. It seems the damage is long-lasting, as Chorley was sent to St Mungo's Hospital for Magical Maladies and Injuries to recuperate. This is likely due to the fact powerful, dark magic may leave irreversible biological damage, such as when George had his ear cursed off permanently. Hand Movement: Point wand at victim; Incantation: Imperio (im-PEER-ee-oh); Effect: Total control over the victim." Quote Source: https://harry-potter-compendium.fandom.com/wiki/Imperius_Curse

5th Degree Rape AKA Consensual Rape =
Intimately inserting yourself into someone whose consent is rendered invalid due to their being either too mentally or emotionally underdeveloped, uninformed, misinformed, barely conscious, or otherwise incapable of processing the situation properly. Unwanted hypnotism or uninvited types of hypnotism are also included in this category.

The terms "rape" and "rapist" usually depicted or written in this book are meant to reflect 3rd and/or 4th-degree types of rape-- NOT 1st or 2nd degree. However, the term "rape" used to describe what the character "DeVille" represents in the series Virgins vs Aliens: Prom King   is indeed actually referring to 1st and 2nd-degree rape.

Tally ho, noble warriors! Tally ho!

"Voldemort raised his wand, and before Harry could do anything to defend himself before he could even move, he had been hit

again by the Cruciatus curse. The pain was so intense, so all-consuming, that he no longer knew where he was... white-hot knives were piercing every inch of his skin, his head was surely going to burst with pain; he was screaming more loudly than he'd ever screamed in his life." —
HARRY POTTER UNDER THE EFFECTS OF THE CURSE

--That's also how the presidential fraternity / deep state cult made me feel every month for years, off and on, for 12 Years A Slave to their pain porn show, which I was 10 years a publicly viewable sharecropper for without my knowledge or consent-- as I was exploited on their publicly visible dark web underground live stream of me since I was a 14-year-old minor in 1999-- and before that it was a secretly passcode-accessed child exploitation live stream show that they'd imprisoned me on, since I was born, going from a randomly older-peer-child-predatory version of The Truman Show during my childhood, to a mostly Mary Tyler Moore Show version of The Truman Show when I started working full-time jobs, to an abruptly Pan's Labyrinth version of The Truman Show, for the past 12 years (since 2009), gradually increasing in intensity and horror, from my perspective. I'm told people saw me naked even when I was 14, but I didn't know this until 22 years later.

Also, the mother in my story, "The Superhero Rape Experiment" is the depiction of a clone of my mom irl-- one who has been "under the imperious curse" of consciousness override by a myriad of different people each day-- and-- as it thankfully turns out-- is not my actual mother.

<u>NOW-- from what I understand:</u>

The Clintons and The Trumps are responsible for starting this whole mess, back in 1999, in order to profit off of exploiting me and depriving me, while abusing me, assaulting me and intimately violating me with violently painful bioterrorism brutality, brain rape assault, and other forms of torture and domineering violence under the guise of "clinical trials" I knew nothing about-- a variety of methods to try to figure out how to control me, usurp my power and steal my wealth (both of which no one bothered to inform me of the existence of until this year), while trying to piss me off until I chose to become the leader of 1 of their 2 sides, to stop them and virtually spank them for pissing me off and hurting me.

And they've had a big bet going for years on which type of leader I'd choose to be over them-- either the original plan to make me POTUS, or the 2nd idea, which came later, to make me NSA.

After seeing how many ways they intended to further destroy me and whatever future personal life I might barely feign to have as their PTSD'd leader-- all in their desperately sociopathically gollum-eyed control freak supremacy hopes of gruesomely controlling me while I'm in office-- either office-- as they have been desperate to not only control me and my power-- but to also keep my extreme wealth in house-- I instead declined both sides, refusing both offers to be their leader, including their presidential show pony voodoo doll spy slave in chief (or presidential show pony voodoo doll spy slave "1st Lady"-- both easily replaced by a clone or a lookalike, according to them), as well as their routinely brutalized Alice in NSA Wonderland: Pan's Labyrinth Nightmare on Live Stream edition.

So I have not chosen to be their leader in any capacity, and I totally intend to escape this vile

country and its vile agents of evil, and take all my
wealth with me-- and my only interest in these
atrociously vicious savages (and the disappointingly
surprising traitors who obeyed them) is to stop their
psychotic physical assault on my body, health,
household and life right now-- and see that they all
either walk the plank soon or soon spend life
incarcerated, be it thawed out behind bars for the
rest of their lives, or frozen in cryogenics chambers
for 700 years.

I WILL NEVER GIVE THEM WHAT THEY WANT AND
THEY WILL NEVER WIN ANYTHING. EVER. THEY ALL
TOTALLY LOST, THEY ALL TOTALLY FAILED AND ALL
OF THEIR VILLAINS AND ALL OF THEIR MINIONS AND
ALL OF THEIR BOSSES ARE ALL GOING TO PLEAD
GUILTY-- THOSE WHO SURVIVE --THE RECKONING.

This 8yr "2-term whitehouse" clinical trial run of
socially testing my reactions to social emotional
cerebral spiritual financial medical trauma &
ulcer-inducing change while on their violent mind
control chemical (w/out my knowledge or consent)
began 12/6/2010 (my 25th birthday) which makes sense
cause I was repeatedly told this year that all this was
originally meant to be over 12/6/2018 (8yrs) but
because I wasn't 'controllable' the sick freaks trying to
break me like a 🐎 horse extended their deadline to
Summer 2019.

Then 12/6/19.

Then Summer 2020.

Then 12/6/20.

Then Summer 2021.

Then 12/6/21.

But I'm obviously still not 'controllable' as I've brazenly flouted everyone & everything, even making jaded spies bum out, questioning their skills, cause even after years of their efforts-- I still refuse to let anyone in or pretend this is anything more than a ruse to record agenda-driven interactions w/me & I often feel relieved when I no longer feel obligated by my own social courtesy to pretend they're anything but a programmed data extractor for their bosses who are the infuriating bane of my existence.

Tho it coulda been 12/6/09 when the 8yr Whitehouse clinical trials began, making 12/6/17 the original end date, which makes even more sense, cause not only did I get a bit of funding 12/6/09, but 2017 was the year Bailey set me up to pretend I was crazy just so he could lock me up in a mental hospital ward, further test their chemical on me in a concentrated, lab-rat-in-a-cage way & pretend they made progress in making me crack-- to justify extending the original 12/6/17 deadline end of their vile disgusting presence in my life.

So really by all these villains' own terms-- this whole thing was actually spose to be over *4* yrs ago on 12/6/17. They used bs tactics to keep me longer.

So why should I believe a promise of 12/6/21? They already hinted @ Summer 2022!

Their word has been garbage.

But it'll be alright-- because the NEW FBI and the NEW Homeland Security will fix all that-- *and you*-- *for good*-- *for the good of us all.*

So I know what I am and I know what I'm not. You can keep saying I'm your president all you want-- but if it were true-- if I really *was* your president-- you would treat me better, with dignity and honor-- like you do for some of my apparently "bystander effected" live stream exploitation viewers. Or you would at *least* have a healthy *fear* of my *power* and my *wrath*.

And you would *know* that I deserve *respect*.

Not constant **assault, brutality,** and *pain*.

So obviously-- by evidence of your own irreverently cruel disregard for:

☐ my basic human rights,
☐ my entire adult existence and
☐ my soul's fast-emptying tank of humanity--

I AM NOT YOUR POTUS-- to bioterrorize, Oculus drug, try to hypnotize, exploit and then replace with a clone as soon as it finally hits you that you CAN'T override my consciousness. I AM NOT THAT PRESIDENT. Nor have I chosen anyone to *be* your president-- because I would never *be* or *choose* a president before I was:

- ❖ _physically free_ from *ALL* potential bioterrorism,
- ❖ _socially free_ to meet and mingle with whomever I choose-- NOT INUNDATED WITH ALL OF THE IMPOSTERS *PRETENDING* TO BE THEM-- and
- ❖ _financially free_ to move out of my house and never again live with any clones, traitors, or consciously overridden spies in disguise insulting me with never-ending lies-- or whatever creepy messed up crap this is here-- ever again.

SO ALL MY THREATS LOST THEIR _BETS_--
       --BECAUSE OF THEIR _BIOTERRORISM_.
Your game of crimes in overtime--
       --is _done_, like I am. _NOW *YOU'RE* IN PRISON_.

Dear Everybody:
(Urgent)

I've been trying all this year thru both 🤚 snail mail and email letters to compel the FBI and Homeland Security to rescue me from the violent brutality and painful assault of The Deep State and the CIA/NSA/POTUS FRAT villains that it seems to run, to no apparent avail.

So if you know anyone who works for the FBI or Homeland Security, please direct them to read what's at my link www.TinyURL.com/DearHomelandSecurity and then contact higherpowerpublishing@gmail.com for more insight and if they have any instructions to have delivered to me through there.

I never know for sure when my correspondence has been compromised, so they may have to try hard to get through to me, in case federally funded hackers try to block them-- including my multiple-personalities-disorder-acting housemate who "doesn't believe in bureaucracy" and never once bought me any health insurance to keep me healthy and alive, but for some odd reason took out a life insurance policy on me, which she never fails to pay-- like it's her religion-- while ignoring all of the cripplingly painful assault, violent bioterrorism and abusive violations I've endured for 12 to 22 to 30 years, under her roof, including physical brutality against me whenever I've tried to run away from this hell, like in 2007, 2010, 2011, 2017 and 2021, and intentionally sabotaging my health and immediate finances, while hiding my wealth from me, in order to keep me too poor to move out and separate myself from her, because she gets kickbacks for being my only handler, babysitter and glorified prison warden.

I no longer consider her my mother-- because she is a clone, and I will no longer be living with my mother's clone-- by no later than new year's day of 2022, but preferably by thanksgiving of 2021, since I've been too broken by her boss's vicious savage bioterrorism these past 2 weeks to make my original Halloween deadline.

All of the FBI and Homeland Security agents who've watched this go on for months, if not years, and done nothing about it-- are all going to Guantanamo Bay prison by the time I'm done with them.

So let me know if you know anybody I don't who will try harder to put a real end to all of this evil abuse and torture once and for all-- cryogenics chambering all of my-- and my 🐾 dog's-- abusers, assaulters, bioterrorists, brain rapists and other violators and torturers who perhaps don't deserve to die-- and putting all the rest-- all the worst-- including all their vicious bosses and savage bosses' bosses, etc-- all on death row-- to fry under the brain-fricasseeing metal hat of their electric chair.

I look forward to *THEIR* unwanted live stream of that chapter in their helpless lives as I eat *MY* popcorn 🍿 flashing *MY* haughtily insensitive pompous arrogance and laughing grin at *THEIR* pain, suffering, misery and agony, and place *MY* bets on them, gambling on whether or not they piss their pants or crap their pants as everybody watches them take their last painful-- and painfully humiliated-- breath...

So if you can get a message on my behalf through to somebody you know in the FBI or The Department of Homeland Security-- that'd be SUPER great-- THANKS A BUNCH!! ⚫👍⚫ Stay #Blessed! 🔔

All FBI and Homeland Security agents who just watch the CIA POTUS FRAT NSA Deep State cult assault me with violent bioterrorism and they do nothing to stop it-- you are probably not gonna make it out alive from Guantanamo Bay prison. Neither are the traitors who I trusted to have my back who instead felt like ignoring my pain and/or contributing to it.

My new wealth will give me the power to protect people. But I will not protect those who never bothered to protect me, when they could have-- and should have.

These are most of the names involved in not only the severely painful vicious savage cruel and unusual criminal assault on my body, brain, family, pet and life-- but also on others, as allegedly led or "controlled" (paid, consciousness overridden, Oculus mind-controlled, intimidated, threatened, directed) by "Donald Trump Jr", "Robert Trump", "Bill Clinton" and/or "Hilllary Clinton": Spy aliases who work for the POTUS families they proxy for and/or impersonate:

George Washington, Martha Washington, John Adams, Abigail Adams, Thomas Jefferson, Aaron Burr, George Clinton, James Madison, Dolley Madison, Elbridge Gerry, James Monroe, Elizabeth Kortright Monroe, Daniel D. Tompkins, John Quincy Adams, Louisa Catherine Adams, John C. Calhoun, Andrew Jackson, Rachel Jackson, Martin Van Buren, Hannah Hoes Van Buren, Richard M. Johnson, William Henry Harrison, Anna Tuthill Symmes Harrison, John Tyler, Letitia Christian Tyler, Julia Gardiner Tyler, James K. Polk, Sarah Childress Polk, George M. Dallas, Zachary Taylor, Margaret Mackall Smith Taylor, Millard Fillmore, Abigail Powers Fillmore, Franklin Pierce, Jane M. Pierce ,William R. King, Franklin Pierce, Jane M. Pierce, James Buchanan, John C. Breckinridge, Abraham Lincoln, Mary Todd Lincoln, Hannibal Hamlin,

Andrew Johnson, Eliza McCardle Johnson, Ulysses S. Grant, Julia Dent Grant, Schuyler Colfax, Henry Wilson, Rutherford Birchard Hayes, Lucy Webb Hayes, William A. Wheeler, James A. Garfield, Lucretia Rudolph Garfield, Chester A. Arthur, Ellen Lewis Herndon Arthur, Grover Cleveland, Frances Folsom Cleveland, Thomas A. Hendricks, Benjamin Harrison, Caroline Lavinia Scott Harrison, Mary Lord Harrison, Levi P. Morton, Adlai E. Stevenson, William McKinley, Ida Saxton McKinley, Garret A. Hobart, Theodore Roosevelt, Edith Kermit Carow Roosevelt, Charles W. Fairbanks, William H. Taft, Helen Herron Taft, James S. Sherman, Woodrow Wilson, Ellen Axson Wilson, Edith Bolling Galt Wilson, Thomas R. Marshall, Warren G. Harding, Florence Kling Harding, Calvin Coolidge, Grace Goodhue Coolidge, Charles G. Dawes, Herbert Hoover, Lou Henry Hoover, Charles Curtis, Franklin D. Roosevelt, Eleanor Roosevelt, John N. Garner, Henry A. Wallace, Harry S. Truman, Bess Wallace Truman,

Alben W. Barkley, Dwight D. Eisenhower,

Mamie Doud Eisenhower, Richard M. Nixon,

John F. Kennedy, Jacqueline Kennedy, Lyndon

B. Johnson, Lady Bird Johnson, Hubert H.

Humphrey, Pat Nixon, Spiro T. Agnew, Gerald

R. Ford, Betty Ford, Nelson Rockefeller,

Jimmy Carter, Rosalynn Carter, Walter F.

Mondale, Ronald Reagan, Nancy Reagan,

George H.W. Bush, Barbara Bush, Dan

Quayle, Bill Clinton, Hillary Rodham Clinton,

Albert Gore, George W. Bush, Laura Bush,

Richard Cheney, Barack Obama, Michelle Obama,

Joseph R. Biden, Donald J. Trump, Melania Trump,

Mike Pence, Jill Biden Kamala Harris--

or any 1st or 2nd Family Children, Grandchildren,

Brothers, Sisters, Aunts, Uncles, or other 1st or 2nd

Family relatives-- along with a litany of celebrity impersonators of public figures and private citizens or civilians in my life-- who all lost, who all failed, and of whom all villains who survived pleaded guilty.

Other Names

involved in all this abusive assault, bioterrorism brutality, violent violation, and perverse pain have also included:

The insinuation that Reed Henrikson is actually Donald Trump Jr while Donald Trump Jr is actually Tom Ridley Jr. Allegedly, all the "Trumps" are actually Ridleys and all those abstract names like the savage Cory Manning (Robert Trump), Maynard Rawley (Barron Trump), Yvonne Muri (Ivanka Trump), Mads Eade (Donald Trump Sr)-- and the entire Bryce family-- are also all really The Trumps. Why So Serious about having so many decoy proxies to hide behind, Trumps? FYI-- whether or not the Trump code names are real or just another BS excuse to get out of facing the consequences for all of their crimes-- I BELIEVE that: Donald Trump Jr (Tom Ridley Jr and Henrikson) is worse than Bill Clinton is worse than Robert Trump (Manning) is worse than Hillary Clinton is worse than Donald Trump Sr. (Eade) is worse than Bill Clinton Jr. is worse than The REAL Eric Trump (Bailey) is worse than Chelsea Clinton is worse than Ivanka Trump (Muri) is worse than Chelsea's kid(s) is worse than Barron Trump (Rawley). And Tiffany's not actually related, she's more like Malania, in a childbride of Robert sort of way-- but Tiffany's guilty too, as guilty as Chelsea is. And Malanias guilty too, as guilty as Chelsea's kid(s) are.

**NOW EXPOSE ALL RAPES/CRIMES, SECRETS & IDENTITIES OF-- & CRYOGENICS CHAMBER FOR 1,000 YEARS UNDER THE OCEAN SEA OR IN OUTER SPACE ALL OF THESE SERIAL BIOTERRORISTS OF MINE:**

1. Don Trump Jr AKA "President Snow" of The Hunger Games (serial child rapist/cryogenics-chamber-into-outer-space-for-1,000-yearser who has tried to make people cryogenics-chamber-in-outer-space me, REAL Dustin Fallriver of *NSTED, and other innocent people)

2. Hillary Clinton AKA Hannah Rose AKA Mrs. Hawthorne AKA "President Coin" of The Hunger Games (serial consciousness-override-rapist-of-minors)
3. Rob Trump (serial child rapist/cryogenics-chamber-into-outer-space-for-1,000-yearser)
4. Bill Clinton AKA Morgan Freeman AKA Nick Hawthorne (serial cryogenics-chamber-into-outer-space-for-1,000-yearser "avatared-to-rape" by Don Jr)
5. Freddy "Krueger" Trump (The 2nd)-- allegedly already dead but let's make 100% sure
6. Bill Clinton's Brother Jeff Dwire*
7. Don Trump Sr (serial cryogenics-chamber-into-outer-space-for-1,000-yearser; murdered my grandma; "avatared-to-rape" by Don Jr)
8. Bill Clinton's Father William Jefferson Blythe Jr.*
9. Freddy Trump The 3rd
10. Melania Trump
11. All the other Clintons and Trumps who've repeatedly plotted to initiate harming me
12. Reed Henrikson AKA 44's Sick Evil Clone (serial rapist of women who mistook him for 44 + plotted to take REAL Dustin Fallriver of *NSTED's life to punish him for me liking JT more)
13. Jonathan Bailey AKA _FORMER_ CIA Director John Ritter (3X cryogenics-chamber-into-outer-space-for-1,000-yearser who raped teens)
14. Emma Thompson

15. Jessica Biel

16. Sonia Bryce

17. Richard Bryce

18. Noah Bryce

19. Cory Manning

20.   Maynard Rawley

21. Yvonne Muri

22.   Mads Eade

23.   FBI-Infamous Serial Rapist, Child Violator, Sex Trafficker & Murderer Ted Davidoff

24.   Every person who has ever pretended to be a member of a presidential family-- or any other political figure pretender, proxy, decoy, impersonator and/or clone (immediately cryogenics all of these people right now-- and keep them cryogenics chambered under the ocean indefinitely, for years, until they are in position to shuttle to outer space).

25.   Whoever keeps making clones of us.

26.   All The Interactive Psychotic Viewers of The Live-Streamed Prison of Pain-Porn Creepshow that I have been an abused, tortured, violated, exploited, enslaved prisoner of since 1999-- & my informant has all of their names & addresses, amounting to a grand total of my now 9,772 rapey-torture attempted murderers

27. And any other threat or dangerous enemy, like anyone who willfully tried to destroy me or my loved ones or nefariously control my life or my loved ones or experiment on me or my loved ones (including doing uninvited, unwanted, unknown, untested clinical trials on us-- even on celebs like Keanu Reeves & Colin Farell)

without our knowledge or consent or block my success
in order to oppress me or rob me or rape my rights-- &
anyone else who has ordered or otherwise initiated
pain, deprivation, bioterrorism, critter terrorism, poison,
sickness, health sabotage, numbness, brain fog, fatigue,
fat, death, sexual assault, some type of rape, or any
other bad, awful, painful, negative, disabling,
sabotaging, terrorizing, torturing, crippling,
debilitating, violating, imprisoning, restricting, blocking,
dehumanizing, abusive or otherwise unwanted thing to
be done to me, my life or any being in my home, in my
core nucleus, or on my side), but especially anyone who
tried to override, control, replace or mess up me or
mine.

- SERIAL ANIMAL/BIO-TORTURERS GET CRYOGENICS
  CHAMBERED 100 YEARS.
- FIRST TIME BIO-VIOLATORS GET CRYOGENICS
  CHAMBERED FOR 10 YEARS.
- BAKER ACT FOR 1-WEEK ANYONE WHO VIOLATES MY
  HOME (FAMILY, PET, HOUSE/SPACE) OR
  PERSON/BODY/BRAIN: EVERY SINGLE TIME THEY
  MENACE ME-- MENACE THEM BACK W/A FULL WEEK AT
  A LITERALLY CRAPPY NUTHOUSE;

_PLACE IN BIBLE-BASED HEALTH & WELLNESS
RETREATS FORMER SERIAL BIOTERRORISTS OF MINE,
INCLUDING:_

1. Ivanka Trump
2. Tiffany Trump
3. Chelsea Clinton & Her Kid(s) (who helped her father try to cryogenics-chamber-in-outer-space me by bioterrorizing the hell out of my back, doubling me over in crippling pain, in order to get me to pop the pain pills that her dad, "Bill Clinton", poisoned while I was taking a bath)
4. PiNK!
5. Zoe Kravitz
6. KeKe Palmer
7. Oprah
8. Tyler Perry
9. Chris Rock
10. Bill Gates
11. T.I.
12. Jeff Bezos
13. Idris Elba
14. Warren Buffett
15. Will Smith
16. Trevor Noah's clones
17. Eric Trump
18. J.R. Kirby
19. & Everyone Else Who Violated Me But Doesn't Deserve A Cryo Life-Shelfing

It would appear that all of these people (and/or their impersonators-- or both, most likely) made a dirty deal with the devils in the NSA/CIA/Deep State cult-- and yes, I'm including at least some of the actual 1st families that some, most or all of these people have impersonated.

Nobody has yet walked away from this clean-- from what I can tell-- not even my own mother-- who either abandoned me due to being kidnapped and replaced by a clone-- or who betrays me on the regular because these monsters hijacked her headspace and refuse to let her go-- like a cult that ruins every person and every thing that it touches.

The Deep State Cult is akin to amoral, sociological leprosy.

They have needlessly preyed on the weakest, most vulnerable and most helpless members of our society like demons looking for a pure soul to vilely suck the life out of.

If they turned out to be devil worshippers it would NOT surprise me AT all, but rather it would confirm my suspicions about them each being the devil's bitch.

They hijacked my illegally live streamed life and criminally tried to control my life, power and finances-- even if it meant crippling my health, family, pets, social life, planned career as a filmmaker/author/soundtrack singer/songwriter, etc-- and all of my basic human rights, since the year 1999-- excluding the years before that when I was child exploited without my knowledge by the previous former power that came before the latest one(s).

Their evil plot has put me in the hospital on multiple occasions due to their intensely cripplingly painful assault, violent bioterrorism and other perverse brutality and abusive violations-- but most especially every time I've ever tried to run away (like in 2007, 2010, 2011, 2017, and 2021).

Members of the FBI and Homeland Security have been watching all this-- some, I'm told, for many years--

anywhere from just this year all the way to 16 years ago
(2005)-- if not before then.

I have not accepted any proposed leadership roles from
these people, as no one formally offered me anything. They
just whisper weird, random impressions of ideas to me
through muted signals I see and "secretly coded" bull shit I
read or watch.

They've been trying to violate me into feeling obligated to
be their leader just to get from under their thumbs and
eliminate everyone who abused me or ordered or
orchestrated my abuse.

Meanwhile, there's a potentially legitimate cover story
that's been at play for years, about me being the
unconsenting, unknowing human bio-psychophysiological
experiment of FDA NON-APPROVED, untested,
unsanctioned, UNSAFE clinical trials, to test their violent
mind control chemical, "Oculus" out on me.

It looks to me like all of it is true.

But because I never accepted their "leadership"-- I'm just
an ordinary private citizen whom they and their stupid BS
"algorythm" OF HUMAN STAFF WORKERS-- have chosen to
abusively violate, violently bioterrorize, painfully assault,
and otherwise harm the body, brain and life of-- making
me a public figure to the dark web underworld of spy
culture-- without my knowledge or consent-- by ruining my
life-- my adulthood, my health and my financial access-- on
a secret live stream I never knew about or condoned--
which they all became billionaires off of, while I've had only
61 cents in the bank account I have access to-- still not yet
compensated for the crimes against me that everybody

else profited off of-- as they destroyed all of my
relationship circles in the process.

They've taken most everything I've said out of context on
purpose-- intentionally twisting my usually positive good
intent meaning into something vile, cruel, often to harm
me, and they've hidden from me both my 22 to 30 to 36 year
reparations, and non-psycho, non-villainous supporters
and/or friends and family.

They've been guilty of kidnapping, torture, gambling on
their kidnapped torture victim(s?), murdering innocent
people, knowingly grand theft robbing innocent people,
and some, like people who call themselves "Clintons" or
"Trumps" have also been guilty of serial rape, child
molestation, pedophilia, and other forms of assault,
including but not limited to severely painful bioterrorism
(3rd degree rape), brain rape (4th degree), and other
violent violations and abuse.

All of the FBI and Homeland Security agents who let all
this go down on their watch will now be put behind the
bars of Guantanamo Bay prison, for aiding and abetting
all these villains and their villainy for 16 to 22 to 30+ years
of crime against me and others-- by not doing their jobs to
stop it.

They will immediately and permanently be replaced by
agents who do and will do their jobs to shut down this
nightmare on live stream, instantly stop all of the
bioterrorism and painfulness I've been put through-- and
eliminate all the demons who worked so hard at trying to
harm me, assault me, etc.

Immediately and permanently detain and eradicate
everyone who has routinely or severely caused any pain,

loss, damage or other cruel bad thing to happen to me or any member of my household-- including my pets.

This includes catching and handling everyone who gambled on any of this with no intent of their bet helping me.

ABOUT 'MOTHER'

Earlier this year, somebody blocked my online and USPS correspondence to the FBI and Homeland Security and pretended to call them for help just so I wouldn't try harder to, once I realized who I could actually call for help-- and once I figured out what to say to help me make sense of it all, as, much of what I've been told to help me understand it all is a bit scattered, fragmented, convoluted, and surreal-- as well as a bit much to grasp...

I affirm this:

> → No more abusive assault!!!!!!!!!!!!!!!!!!!!!!!!
> → No more bioterrorism brutality!!!!!!!!!!!!!!!!!!!!!!!!
> → No more perversely caused pain!!!!!!!!!!!!!!!!!!!!!!!! &
> → No more violent violations!!!!!!!!!!!!!!!!!!!!!!!!

No one will lie to me, hurt me, trick me, harm me, otherwise deceive me, violate me, terrorize me, hustle me, plague me, villainously spy on me-- or block me. From here on out EVERYONE MUST TELL ME THE TRUTH, THE WHOLE TRUTH & NOTHING BUT THE TRUTH-- SO HELP YOU ALL GOD-- AND NEVER VIOLATE ME-- WHICH INCLUDES NEVER ASSAULTING

ME AND NEVER USING VIOLENCE TO
COMMUNICATE WITH ME-- AND YOU ALL NOW GIVE
ME FULL ACCESS TO EVERYTHING AND EVERYONE I
WANT TO ACCESS-- IMMEDIATELY-- AND ALWAYS--
CEASELESSLY AND EASILY.

ALSO-- You will indefinitely, safely, securely, and
privately baker act my mentally ill
mother/"mom-clone"/house-mate right now (as soon
as either "Dustin Fallriver of *NSTED", "Trenton Gates
of BRiDE", and/or "Allen iBang of Fury Planter" are free
and available to either come get me or send for me
and host me indefinitely in their home-- and I can pay
my share of the full rent via my access to my major
financial account(s)-- unless, until or after I get my
own place, which is what I've wanted to do since 2007,
2010, 2011, 2017 and 2021-- all the years I tried to run
away before getting viciously punished for it with both
mental, emotional, spiritual and physical / medical
assault-- but I'd be happy and overjoyed to do it right
now-- if I knew how to access the funds and/or other
resources to do it.

I seriously tried to live on my own over a decade ago
when I preferred living at The Ramada Inn to living
with my mother, but I wasn't able to continue affording
it, so I returned to her home and tried to find more
income-- which I then conveniently got blocked from
finding.

Since I was 18-years-old, my mother has been a
neurologically unwell woman who "doesn't believe in
insurance bureaucracy" and thinks "it's extortion" and
yet she's taken out a never-ending insurance policy
on my life-- and not my health-- just my life-- while not
caring about any of the wretchedly painful abuse,

constant violation, violent assault, traumatic terrorism, and enslaved exploitation I've been enduring for 22 to 30 years while under her roof-- which I have been trying to escape for 14 years-- but medically and financially was repeatedly sabotaged from doing so-- and kept unable to do-- while my possessively controlling and overbearing housemate "mother" has routinely tried to intercept my USPS mail, any people who she's deemed more loyal to me than to her, and my other access to the outside world-- some of which is a federal offense.

How would that make <u>you</u> feel?

The Truth:

My housemate who calls herself my mother is a complete stranger to me.

She is neither my friend, my family, my mentor, my confidante, nor my bank account keyholder. She pretends to be these things in order to be in control of my life and my finances, when in fact, she has been my greatest betrayer, a top facilitator of my greatest pain, assault, abuse, damage, loss, sabotage, and violation-- and I wouldn't trust her with a potted plant let alone anything that means anything to me.

She has behaved like a mindless drone-bot, taking and obeying cruel and horrible orders to harm, abuse, assault, violate, bioterrorize, and otherwise torture both me and my little dogs too, over the past 15 years-- like a Torture DJ, taking requests from villainous scumbags hiding like roaches behind the cloak and dagger shadowy underworld of dark web watching spy culture-- carrying out despicable, villainous orders-- at the touch of a button, by remote control.

She has behaved like a cold-blooded psychopath with multiple personalities disordering her consciousness each and every day. She is evidently unwell-- and clearly unfit to be my handler, babysitter, glorified prison warden-- or bank account keyholder-- as she really needs to be hospitalized in a mental asylum, where she can be observed and perhaps cured.

But either way, it is obvious to anyone and everyone who meets or sees or hears my housemate that she is not fit to have any power, control, or influence over my life-- or the social or financial aspects therein it-- and I will not be living with her after the year 2021.

As soon as humanly possible, I will be living either with friends-- or by myself-- but either way-- my mother and 2020 housemate will not be living with me-- and I will not be living with her. This is the end of us "knowing" each other-- even though neither of us TRULY knows the other-- apparently. If I ever have children-- they will not know their maternal grandmother-- or any of her doppelgangers-- and she/they will not know or be allowed to see them.

<u>*My Winter 2021 Hierarchy of Keyholders*</u>

<u>*is as follows:*</u>

1. My 1st Top Highest Big Bank Account Keyholder = Me-- as recognized by only *MY* original FINGERPRINTS-- AND NOBODY ELSE'S!!!!!!!!!!!!!

~~~~~~

2. My 2nd Highest Big Bank Account Keyholder = My childhood friend Rosie Hatten-- as recognized by only HER original fingerprints-- so long as she never works for any enemy or perceived threat of mine (including any Clinton, Trump, Clinton bot / Trump bot minion, menace-- or anyone else who has ever compelled, ordered or facilitated assaulting me or violating me or harming my household)

~~~~~~

3. My 3rd Highest Big Bank Account Keyholder = My childhood friend Pauline Maxwell-- as recognized by only HER original fingerprints-- so long as she never works for

any enemy or perceived threat of mine (including any
Clinton, Trump, Clinton bot / Trump bot minion, menace--
or anyone else who has ever compelled, ordered or
facilitated assaulting me or violating me or harming my
household)

4. My 4th Highest Big Bank Account Keyholder = My
childhood friend Kathleen Prudent-- as recognized by only
HER original fingerprints-- so long as she never works for
any enemy or perceived threat of mine (including any
Clinton, Trump, Clinton bot / Trump bot minion, menace--
or anyone else who has ever compelled, ordered or
facilitated assaulting me or violating me or harming my
household)

5. My 5th Highest Big Bank Account Keyholder = My
childhood friend Amy Khamphanh-- as recognized by only
HER original fingerprints-- so long as she never works for
any enemy or perceived threat of mine (including any
Clinton, Trump, Clinton bot / Trump bot minion, menace--
or anyone else who has ever compelled, ordered or
facilitated assaulting me or violating me or harming my
household)

6. My 6th Highest Big Bank Account Keyholder = My cousin
Moriah Joy Perkins Fletcher-- as recognized by only HER
original fingerprints-- so long as she never works for any
enemy or perceived threat of mine (including any Clinton,
Trump, Clinton bot / Trump bot minion, menace-- or
anyone else who has ever compelled, ordered or facilitated
assaulting me or violating me or harming my household)

7. My 7th Highest Big Bank Account Keyholder = The Film
Jingle Jangle's Justin Cornwell-- as recognized by only HIS
original fingerprints-- so long as he never works for any
enemy or perceived threat of mine (including any Clinton,
Trump, Clinton bot / Trump bot minion, menace-- or
anyone else who has ever compelled, ordered or facilitated
assaulting me or violating me or harming my household)

8. My 8th Highest Big Bank Account Keyholder = The TV

Series Daily Show's Trevor Noah-- as recognized by only HIS original fingerprints-- so long as he never works for any enemy or perceived threat of mine (including any Clinton, Trump, Clinton bot / Trump bot minion, menace-- or anyone else who has ever compelled, ordered or facilitated assaulting me or violating me or harming my household)

~~~~~~

9. My 9th Highest Big Bank Account Keyholder = The TV Series Roots' Rege-Jean-Page-- as recognized by only HIS original fingerprints-- so long as he never works for any enemy or perceived threat of mine (including any Clinton, Trump, Clinton bot / Trump bot minion, menace-- or anyone else who has ever compelled, ordered or facilitated assaulting me or violating me or harming my household)

~~~~~~

10. My 10th Highest Big Bank Account Keyholder = The TV Series SLiDE's Brenton Thwaites-- as recognized by only HIS original fingerprints-- so long as he never works for any enemy or perceived threat of mine (including any Clinton, Trump, Clinton bot / Trump bot minion, menace-- or anyone else who has ever compelled, ordered or facilitated assaulting me or violating me or harming my household)

~~~~~~

11. My 11th Highest Big Bank Account Keyholder = The Film Harry Potter's Alfred Enoch-- as recognized by only HIS original fingerprints-- so long as he never works for any enemy or perceived threat of mine (including any Clinton, Trump, Clinton bot / Trump bot minion, menace-- or anyone else who has ever compelled, ordered or facilitated assaulting me or violating me or harming my household)

~~~~~~

12. My 12th Highest Big Bank Account Keyholder = The Boy Band *NSYNC's Justin Timberlake-- as recognized by only HIS original fingerprints-- so long as he never works for any enemy or perceived threat of mine (including any Clinton, Trump, Clinton bot / Trump bot minion, menace-- or anyone else who has ever compelled, ordered or facilitated assaulting me or violating me or harming my household)

~~~~~~
~~~~~~

NOTE:

<u>*ALL PETS ARE INCLUDED AS PART OF MY "HOUSEHOLD".*</u>

I put the people I've actually met over the people I haven't because I can easily readily identify them face to face, whereas I don't know where the others actually are, if they actually know who I am, let alone where I am, and every marriable bachelor I've named has suddenly become impersonated by a flurry of "clones", TV lookalikes, personality imitators and other fraudulent imposters who I know are not them-- but who keep standing in the way between me and Justin-- or me and Brent-- or me and Alfred-- or me and literally every heartthrob I've ever thought to mention-- which means (it ***appears*** that) none of them are truly accessible to me without a bunch of fake-ass doppleganger bull shit artists crowding up the stadium between us-- until *AFTER I MOVE OUT OF THIS HOUSE.*

Then I will have no traitorous handler, sabotage-centric babysitter, glorified prison warden, or jock-blocking gatekeeper-- who deludes herself into thinking she's my "mother"-- to trick, trap, torture DJ, and use me every day to practice all of her "Justin Timberlake" impressions, and "Brenton Thwaites" impressions, and "Alfred Enoch" impressions on.

I will be alone-- and ready to access everything and everyone who apparently has been accessing me for dozens of years.

The girls listed are by order of who seems the most accessible to me down to who seems the least accessible to me by distance and communication.

The boys listed are by order of who seems to have disappointed me the least down to who seems to have disappointed me the most, in the storm of all this new bioterrorism assault and violent violation and painful abuse that seemed recharged against me this month, even if it seems unfair to charge that to unofficial civilians, due to most people having limited power.

But all of you had the power to call for help.

And keep calling.

Until you finally reached somebody in the FBI or Homeland Security who's NOT a frat-bot cult-brainwashed asshole-- who would actually be a hero-- MERELY BY DOING THEIR JOB THAT THEY GET PAID EVERY DAY TO DO-- and help you help me escape this criminal community and its cruel and usual kidnapping, controlling, torturing, and strategic ruining of me.

So perhaps you were never really there to begin with.

Or perhaps you got tricked into thinking it was over, and that this was just a waiting game now-- until my birthday.

Then it's time to renew my faith in old childhood friends and "fam", who I can actually see with my eyes, directly-- face to face-- even in my own house-- or at their job down the street-- who I can get the impression of a direct response from on my phone:

★ Like Rosie, who lives a carefree life of limited responsibilities, and is always available to help me-- even recently bringing me food to my house-- previously picking up my medical prescriptions and crowdfunding her church to financially help me out-- and I can track her down at her church if ever I lost her number.
★
★ Or Pauline, who works right across from where I donate, and who is glad I still care, doesn't want to lie to me now-- or have any issues between us-- and in addition to her previously helping me with food, money, and birthday surprises-- I get the impression she's responsible with budgeting.
★
★ Or Kathleen, who lives right down the street from me, and who is looking for a job from me-- and she knows something about Mr. Timberlake's alleged entry into my life

over the past 5 years-- which I'm curious to learn.

★

★ Or Amy, who allegedly lives out of state, but who has also always been both materially giving and responsive-- easy to get a hold of-- and who would NEVER sleep with a guy whom she believed was intended for me.

★

★ Or Riah, who also allegedly lives out of state, but who wants to talk with me, knows what's been going on, and recently helped me out with food assistance, and who is related to me by blood-- in case the person with whom I need to replace my "mother" needs to share my DNA to qualify-- MORIAH **_DOES_**.

★

**So all i's have been dotted, all t's have been crossed off the list, and all boxes have been checked for me to be a separate household from my housemate "mother's" household-- and move forward with all of the previously mentioned names as my support system and banking buddies.**

Now-- I've been given the impression that:

- Rosie has been employed by Barack Obama's representative, Jonathan "Eric Trump/Dennis Ridley" Bailey (or something like that),
- Pauline-- who was once under the same employ 5 years ago-- has more recently been employed by Bill Clinton's representative,
- Kathleen has been employed by Hillary Clinton's representative,
- Amy has been employed by Donald or Robert Trump's representative,
- and Riah has been employed by The Obamas' representative(s)--

--while some of her family members, like Rachel, were allegedly representing my dog Freddy's murderer-- Hillary Clinton's representative-- hence why I did not include Rachel and a few others, back when I was playing the fantasy football version of dream-casting what my ideal

CIA hierarchy of authority would look like-- especially if it meant stopping all the pain, assault and violent abuse of my body, brain, and pet that have plagued my existence.

NONE OF THESE PEOPLE WORK FOR CLINTON, TRUMP, BAILEY, OR ANYONE ELSE WHO HAS EVER ASSAULTED ME, VIOLATED ME, OR OTHERWISE ABUSED THEIR POWER OVER ME.

*THEY NO LONGER HAVE TO ANSWER TO ANY OF THESE MONSTER-FRAUD "PEOPLE"-- AND THEY WILL RECEIVE THE SAME PAY FROM *MY* "BIG BANK ACCOUNT" THAT THEY WERE RECEIVING FROM THEIR FORMER EMPLOYERS, AS MY ACCOUNT SUPERVISORS WHO WILL HELP ME MOVE OUT OF THE HOUSE IN WHICH I CURRENTLY RESIDE, MOVE INTO A NEW ONE I LIKE-- IN A WHEATHER/TEMPERATURE-PERFECT AREA I LOVE-- AND ACCESS MY LOOOOOOOOOOOOONG OVERDUE REPARATION FUNDS-- SO I MAY FINALLY START MY LIFE-- WHICH WAS STUNTED AND RUINED BY ALL THESE CRAZY POLITICAL SPY PEOPLE AND ALL THEIR CRAZY POLITICAL SPY WHITEHOUSE CLINICAL TRIAL EVILLY VICIOUSLY SOCIOPATHIC AND STUPIDLY SAVAGELY PSYCHOTIC BULL SHIT.*

You're welcome.

Any way-- here it is-- my most urgent story and future prediction belief of all-- The End of The Game of Crimes and all of its violent violations, perverse pain, bioterrorism brutality and abuse assaults, titled:

<u>The Game of Crimes Is Over (and it will never return).</u>

Degrees of Villainy

(1 being most criminal, 5 being least on this list):

➢ 1. KNOWINGLY Compelling assault of innocents, then not blocking innocents from that assault or violation (because of you)

➢ 2. KNOWINGLY Ordering assault of innocents

➢ 3. KNOWINGLY Carrying out assault of innocents

➢ 4. KNOWINGLY Facilitating assault of innocents

➢ 5. KNOWINGLY Not honestly trying to stop assault of innocents when you know it's your job to

<u>How it started:</u>

1. Before The Presidential Fraternity and/or "Electoral College" voted to keep me their "presidential nominee" back in 2002 (and then again, repeatedly, many times after that, in future years, including 2011 and 2021, I'm told)-- Freddy "Krueger" Trump (The 2nd)-- Donald Trump Sr's dad-- picked me to be a presidential nominee back in 1989, because he liked how rapable I looked as a little baby girl child, after he saw "Don Jr" and Eric avataring-- or just straight up overriding the consciousness of-- my neighbor-- The Boy Next Door (TJ Robinson)-- who was a couple years older than me-- during TJ/Jr's attempts to molest me in my bedroom-- or wherever he could find a private

moment with me-- as Krueger watched me on the secret child predatory centric and privately password-accessible only live stream that I was unknowingly exploited on as a young child. Krueger was secretly dementia-executed by the CIA from 1991 (Freddy's Dead) to 1999, so that he'd forget my face and name before he could ever get the physical opportunity to make his sick pedophile wet dreams come true-- though it's also insinuated that the sick lust to violate me began when I was born in 1984-- which is when A Nightmare On Elm Street was originally released-- as I've come to terms with the concept that the CIA has been using mainstream media-- including most if not all of Hollywood-- to deliver their coded messages to both each other-- and to nominees whom they expect to be POTUS or CIA some day.

2. Since 1999, I was again being violated and exploited without my knowledge on Trump's or Clinton's and/or both CIA/NSA agents' hidden-from-mainstream "dark web live stream"-- which made me a publicly known figure to the spy culture underworld-- completely unbeknownst to me, during their now 22-year Deep State plot to usurp my power, control my wealth, and exploit my marital sex life in the future, by way of planning to put me in a politically arranged marriage with a consciousness overrideable mate, who they could charge all the perverted billionaires in their rolodex top dollar to avatar (to upload their consciousness into his headspace of and see {through my would-be husband's eyes} me naked in our wedding bed as we were to make love-- which, allegedly, is the reason why Justin Timberlake got cut from being my arranged winner for 1st Man husband-to-be, back in 2000-- and was offered to play 2nd fiddle to his knock-off lookalike, who was

consciousness overridable-- unlike Timberlake-- who was not: #iDontWannaBeTheLoserInThisGameForTwo-- meaning 2 guys and me-- as it was always planned to be a love (avatarable sex) triangle between me and 2 guys). Justin was, perhaps, always intended to be 1 of those 2 guys-- because of my ecstatic fangirl love and fond sentimental memories of him in my favorite boy band of all times-- *NSYNC. Tho, I did like BSB too. ;)

3. In 2006 an alleged clone of my mother began bioterrorizing me, to commercially showcase and test drive on visible live stream for everyone to see-- every sociopathic creatant's ability to pay top dollar to "Brutalize A President" or "Torture The 1st Female POTUS" or "Bio-Rape The Queen"-- for 3 easy payments of-- whatever billionaire club freaks pay to let their scumbag flag fly sky high-- too often at poorer and slave-trafficked or otherwise kidnapped victims' expense.

4. Then in 2009, they began ruining, crippling and sabotaging my health, social circles of trust, and life in general-- with accelerated gusto, after I showed my die hard support for Barack Obama (their obviously biggest competition for dominating claim over my life and future-- and thus my wealth, power and ability for them to sexually and violently exploit for profit-- which they would all then lose-- because of my political career being mutually claimed-- by one President Barack Obama). But I don't think it was just my side that freaked them out and made them lose their sh*t, trying to suddenly destroy me at an abruptly increased intensity. I believe it was PBO-- who saw my excited support and commitment to his presidency, especially after I voluntarily opened up a grassroots headquarters for his campaign in my city, back in 2008-- and they discovered that he had decided that he wanted to professionally work with me-- somebody

he viewed as on his side. They saw him beginning to claim me away from their clutches.

5. But PBO trusted the wrong people to prep me for their political narrative of my life-- an obligatory ritual for becoming POTUS. He entrusted my welfare to the minions of villains who wanted to screw up his plans-- so that they could continue theirs-- all at my expense. Basically, he employed the very people who worked directly for both his and my enemies-- my strategically exploiting violators-- without knowing it-- and tasked them with the mission of preparing me for a political path (an engineered narrative) that he most likely assumed I'd want because of all my political activity between 2008 and 2015.

6. So these people-- many of whom may have even been fond of PBO, as many of them still seem now-- were all led to unknowingly contradict the core purpose of PBO's intent, because their boss(es) (my mortal enemies) villainously plotted to strategically sabotage PBO-- always at my expense-- by having them do the exact opposite of all they should do with me to vet, prep and position me-- and in doing so-- ruined my life.

7. So-- quite naturally-- I refused to comply with them in virtually every way, shape, form and fashion, as I was seeing how their presence in my life-- which I started noticing in November 2014-- had become a decisively villainous one, by late 2015 or early 2016, with the bioterrorism, deprivation and thought invasion-- and I was not EVER going to knowingly reward any of these assholes for further destroying my health (medical life), oppressing my wealth (financial life), and intimately violating all of my private and sacred spaces and basic human rights with callous abandon to boot.

8. Eventually, they realized that their strategy wasn't working. It took them 12 LONG YEARS to realize that they had made a grave and vital error with me and the way they went about (mis)handling me-- even though the last 7 of those years were met with me randomly SCREAMING MY HEAD OFF AT THEM in various spurts and spasms of vehemently venomous fury and unbridled rage at their profoundly screwed up, twisted, perversely painful, obscenely violating, and CLEARLY CRIMINAL occupation in my life. So-- like any average employee who doesn't want to get fired (or lose a life-changing bet)-- instead of just admitting they messed up, by pointing the finger of blame at the root-source-culprit supervillains who signed their paychecks-- and "knew where all the bodies were buried"-- they instead chose the CYA option of making a mad dash to haphazardly cover their asses-- by getting every villain they could find to harm me-- so that they could then fault all those (allegedly) "worse" bad guys-- for all of the damage that was done to my body, my mind, my heart, my spirit, my soul, my family, my friendships, my love life, my pets and my originally planned career life in the arts, as a book-to-screenplay writer/filmmaker and movie soundtrack singer/songwriter-- all of which they obliterated my prime young adult years of, by arrogantly occupying my entire adulthood with all their senseless, assbackwards, counterproductive destruction-- even making up boogeymen for me and everybody else to fear with this covid nonsense, like "Don Jr" (AKA COVID-19-- because, after my life had already been ruined by these assholes, it didn't dawn on them that any of them were a visceral threat to my life, until "Don Jr" (Donald Trump Jr AKA Tom Ridley Jr) allegedly planned to kill me and/or rape me to death since 2019-- probably after seeing me fantasize quite

frequently about Brenton Thwaites-- who I'm guessing looks nothing like Donald Trump Jr, even though I don't actually know for sure what "Donald Trump Jr" even looks like-- I just know that he's the name that's become branded as the source of my pain-- hence why I've had no objections to his untimely departure-- and would happily greenlight that ish, even if it meant I had to do it myself)-- but alas, I'm still never even 100% sure if "Don Jr" ever even existed, in all this smoke and mirrors hustle con game of cloak and dagger doppleganger shadows and clone-bot impersonating spies in disguise... But if he ever did exist, it's been depicted to me that he died and got replaced by lookalikes back in March of 2021-- and yet still I've been trapped in all this hell and oppressive brutality, assault, pain, abuse, violation, violence, lies and deprivation-- because-- Don Jr or not-- at the end of the day-- all of this seems to really still boil down to sleazy greed and power supremacy-- the typical cliche minucha of every dime-a-dozen gollum-eyed shallow-as-a-kiddy-pool megalomaniac in existence, ever since the dawn of mankind. The problem with all my original assaulters' plans to cover up their asses after following Don Jr or Robert Trump or Bill or Hillary Clinton (or all of them) off the proverbial cliff-- is that it's true now-- that much of the damage to my life that all those villains-- who were baited to harm me-- were baited to do-- they did do. So even though they were compelled villainously to let their inner villain off its leash and show the world their worst side-- they did in fact harm me maliciously, knowing that I was an innocent victim in all this, targeted-- trapped-- and tortured by whoever was behind the wheel of this vilely godforsaken nightmare machine of horrors. So even though the former and recent CIA/NSA/Deep State leadership (in bed with

The Presidential Fraternity) launched this assault and started this brutality and led this abuse and supplied all my former violators with all of the expensively overpriced billion dollar price tag equipment to violate and torture me-- merely for the hell of it-- and not even for any reason deeper than that-- all the people who took that bait still took that bait and preyed upon me-- many of them simply because they could. So then the NSA insiders got to play the role of "the secret informant" like the muted morse codian Alexa version of Charlie from Charlie's Angels, giving me the inside scoop on a bunch of crazy-- and not so crazy people, places, things, ideas and purposes-- as everyone made an ass of themselves, cruelly assaulting, abusing, terrorizing and brutalizing me-- all in the name of shits and giggles and The Oculus Apocalypse violent mind control chemical-- or "consciousness overrides"-- all of which I have yet to verify the relevance of in relation to all of the pain and suffering I have endured from all of this blatant evil and flagrantly wicked inhumanity. And I assure you that the only "algorithm" responsible for any of this-- is HUMAN.

9. After they successfully depicted to me how perverted, poisoned, and painfully undermined a presidency would look like in the climate of all this despicably demonic supervillain culture (in effort to win their bet to keep me on their side in the NSA/CIA rather than to follow their original course of instruction, to release me to the presidential fraternity, so that I would instead be one of them)-- I determined that their brand of POTUS was never-- and would never be-- for me-- especially when I felt very potently that I had nobody reliable to ever have my back-- as evidenced by the fact that nobody has yet shown me that they have ever had my back-- other than Justin

Timberlake hooking me up with KDP back in 2016 (with which, unfortunately, the generation of best results are contingent upon who actually is solidified in a position of power in the CIA/NSA to interpret)-- and Alfred Enoch making 1 phone call to the FBI on my behalf, because he feared that someone was about to try to (1st degree) rape me. Otherwise-- I feel alone in a tsunami storm with nothing but a tiny lifeboat and newfangled high-tech paddles that appear to have smacked me in the face by enemy navigation "ghosts in the machine" more times than they've actually ever helped me steer my little boat. So quite naturally that's the time when I get word that my "top secret informant"-- Dennis "Eric Trump" Ridley-- had allegedly been the one who had chosen me, in 2020, to be the next new NSA leader, after he saw how filthy the NSA was in 2019, and-- I'm guessing moreover-- he saw how devilishly deceitful, depraved and despicably ruthless his/their boss(es) were-- to work hard at quietly destroying an innocent girl's life for 12 years straight-- just to block her from being rescued by somebody else-- somebody who didn't seem to realize, even 12 years later, that she needed to be rescued-- and yet still, he was deemed a threat to the villains who viewed me as their own secret private golden goose-- so they ruined not only my life-- but their own careers and spy code-- first by betraying everyone's root source of guidance-- and then by getting exposed and thus exposing everyone else-- burning like a vampire under the sunlight-- and burning everyone else with them. It's a hot mess. Not even hot. It's a lukewarm mess with cold spots in various places.

10. So then-- allegedly because I believed that everyone had been compelled to harm me out of fear of imminent harm or the intimidating threat of danger to them or their loved ones-- all of these people-- and

God only knows how many others-- were instructed by these vicious villainous savage demon beasts who SOMEBODY should NEVER have given ANY job to, let alone a position as powerful as this one-- to not only brutalize me and my helpless household with bioterrorism-- but to do it with unrelenting intensity, so that it was no longer in brief or fleeting spurts and spasms of random bioterrorism brutality, or for 1 guaranteed set of time of daily abusive assault-- as gruesomely engineered and disgustingly carried out by them-- 1 week out of every month-- but this was all day every day in a way that prevented me from even walking without being hunched over on a cane, so not to tip over, during these past few weeks in October of 2021. All just to incriminate my only seeming-friend in all of this-- and to murder my last bit of hope and humanity and relational health-- as now I know I am too damaged for any decent man-- and too disgusted to ever settle for an indecent one. I'm in the Twilight Zone-- unable to "get connected" or "stay connected" with anyone-- even if they weren't a cold and heartless spy just viewing me as a job target mission to trick, use, and abandon with soulless ease. Now I find myself stuck with 1 foot in wanting connection-- and the other foot in hating everything and everyone I would need in order to have any form of connection at all. I want to radically and severely disappear everyone who hurt me off this planet-- and disappear myself off to another country-- where I might actually meet some people who aren't soulless ghouls working for even more soulless ghouls, doing soullessly ghoulish and pointlessly evil crap all because "my spy job told me to do it". I don't love anyone. I don't like anyone. I don't care about anyone. I am numb and lethal with a cold, laser-focused venom that will strike at the least expected moment-- but hopefully right on time-- whenever that time is. Even I don't know. I just know that she's coming. That brimstone and dragon fire "hell hath no fury like a diary of a 'mad Black woman' scorned" streamlined and polished, clear-headed and unfettered-by-emotional-bonds whiplash of catastrophic lightning in me is going to strike-- and going to cause massive wreckage and deep devastation-- and I don't know when, and I don't know how-- I just know-- that I don't and I won't care.

11. Now it's allegedly Team Me4POTUS vs Team Me4NSA because everybody's got a bet going as to which "leadership" option I would choose-- even after both sides betrayed me profoundly and deserve to go to outer space at best-- and walk the plank at worst-- as I just wanna end everyone for having violated me-- relentlessly.

12. So fuck you ALL-- and FUCK YOU very very much.

<u>VINTAGE MADNESS DATA ANALYSIS</u>

A previous notion of who, what, where, why why, and how this all happened is that Robert Trump, Donald Trump Jr, Bill Clinton, Hillary Clinton and others, with the help of Donald Trump Sr and Bill Clinton's rapey son-- and/or their proxy decoys and avatared impersonators-- have all been orchestrating and playing some retardedly messed up Game of Imposters, which I summed up as, "Kill The Decoy" or "How To Get Away With Murdering A Kingmaker / Presidential Nominee / Major Money Mark" (to rob her after violating her for decades-- without leaving any fingerprints-- by manipulating and confusing the hell out of everybody)-- all so they could find and murder whoever they perceived to be an original threat to their power and wealth-- or somebody else's-- and also to try (and fail) to rob me of mine.

Personally, I no longer believe all of these people are the source of all this madness-- but rather they are all just obedient pawns doing what they're told by someone else-- WHEN THEY COULD, SHOULD & NOW GOING FORWARD *WILL* SIMPLY REFUSE *ALL* BAD ORDERS.

I do believe most of them have likely committed heinous crimes of villainy-- or looked the other way and ignored it when someone was doing heinous crimes of vile villainy in their name or face-- but I also believe that they are weak, desperate slaves, who are all just trying to survive a psychotic high stakes game of murder and mayhem, by torturing, raping, killing and destroying others (or trying to)-- all just to entertain the gamblers of the wealthy rich and powerful elite.

I have ended the game and all the torture and evil simply by saying that it is over-- so therefore it is over.

But many people have been under the impression that they would have been murdered by the secret force behind all this-- if they didn't do the bad things they did.

Yet I see no proof that anyone who refused an order actually died.

So I believe this has been a weirdly wicked and wickedly weird "Belief War" / "Bull Shit Contest" / Hustle Con Game of Scams-- to watch desperate decoys, proxies, clones, lookalikes, doppelgangers, impersonators, and other actors scramble like madhatters, doing terrible things (mostly to me) out

of false irrational fear that they would otherwise
perish or be replaced by a clone or something.

If everybody stopped obeying bad orders or other
villainous instructions-- nothing would happen.

No harm would ever come to anyone.

This has been a Shadow Puppet Alice In Wonderland
CIA/NSA Deep State Cult Game of Crimes Stupidity
Showcase for the political elite (or the wealthy
gamblers who control them) to watch and laugh at
how insane/crazy and villainously ruthless everyone
gets when they think they'll die and be replaced by
another version of themselves-- because their lives
don't matter to all of the 'originals' and/or "gamblers"
placing bets on their lives-- and I have been their
publicly live streamed target since 1999-- on a dark
web underworld live stream (as I'm told), in order for
others to try to victimize and violate me into
dysfunction, so others could rob me and control my
life and my presidential/kingmaker power-- while also
trying to get me to kill everybody's decoys just so that
the originals being protected by their "proxies"
(supposedly) would be more killable and more easily
accessible to be killed (I guess).

So I am officially millennially cryogenics chambering
everyone who had anything to do with ordering,
facilitating or carrying out this gruesome psychotic
travesty of humanity and sociopathic mockery of
suffering by innocent people.

No one but the ones truly responsible for this
madness need to die-- and should die-- right now
(which they will). But almost everyone involved does

need to go to outer space and serve time there--
many in their cryogenics chambers for 1,000 years-- so
that NONE of this could POSSIBLY ever happen again
(cause nobody who knows anything about it would
still be here on earth-- except for those who fought it,
soulfully survived it, and were vehemently against it
the whole time). This is what happens now. It will
happen. It is happening. It has happened.

You will end all the monsters who voluntarily / willfully
(and intentionally / knowingly) led people to harm
innocent or undeserving people-- both those who
knowingly started this (allegedly the Trumps-- The
Clintons-- or both)-- and those who knowingly made it
worse (allegedly The Clintons-- or Trumps-- or both).

There are no more proxy decoys for the guilty people
listed by name, alias or crime in this document, until
otherwise specified by me-- starting with every
supervillain and villainous initiator of this evil chaos.

If for any legitimate non-bull-shit-pretentious reason
all proxy decoys must truly be removed on earth in
order for me to "safely" access my people-- and my
funds-- by making innocent or undeserving originals
vulnerable to assassination by "some mysterious bad
guy", then my friends and I will be the ones who take a
trip to outer space for a few years (or months) until
you noble warriors finish stomping out all the roaches
and fleas in the political spy world and beyond-- all of
those who kept trying hard AF to cramp our style.

Thank you and Godspeed-- and you will be greatly
financially rewarded for your work. Also-- just to be on
the safe side-- when I say a person's name I don't
know whether or not it actually means that exact

person or if it's just a decoy, proxy, impersonator or clone who represents that person (or both).

Please Share All This With Every News Media Outlet You Can Find-- and get rewarded for every message you get through to ANY influencer-- on behalf of my freedom from this event in history! I started with this: https://www.angelfire.com/ns2/briancrocker/News_Media_Email_Addresses.htm

...kicking and screaming.

                              HILARY
                  HE DROPPED A HOUSE ON ME!

                        CHILD RAPE VICTIM
                  YOU WANTED IT, LOLITA!

The 14-Year-Old Rape Victim applauds Trump while laughing at awed, livid Hilary, who
is swept away by the FBI and Homeland Security-- along with her daughter Chelsea,
her husband Bill, and his rapey son, "Bill Jr."-- all in disbelief. But then more FBI and
Homeland Security agents swoop down from the ceiling like ninjas, and sweep a very
confused Realtor Don away too, along with his brother Rob, adopted son Jr, and
nephew Rick. The new FBI and Homeland Security agents also arrested some of the
former FBI and Homeland Security agents who were just watching the show casually,
eating popcorn-- not doing their jobs. Then loud, nonstop party bickering commences.
Abe looks confused.

                              ABRAHAM

                  Wait-- what just happened? Who called The

                  FBI and Homeland Security on them?

                              TRUTH

                  Glinda-- The Good Witch. She compelled both

                  The FBI and Homeland Security to imprison all

                  guilty parties, from locking up The Deep State,

                  NSA, CIA, Presidential Fraternity, to locking up

                  all the FBI, Homeland Security, and other law

                  enforcement agents whose lollygagging refusal

to do their jobs gradually became aiding and abetting villainy-- the sorta villainy that violated innocent men, women and children. So their passivity made them complicit accomplices in a lot of politically motivated backroom dark web underworld spy cult crime.

ABRAHAM

Which means?

TRUTH

Which means-- THEY *BOTH* LOST. Actually, literally, ALL of them lost, failed and all villains who survived pleaded guilty. Everybody in The Deep State lost, failed, and all villains who survived pleaded guilty. Everybody in The CIA lost, failed, and all villains who survived pleaded guilty. Everybody in The Presidential Fraternity lost, failed, and all villains who survived pleaded guilty. Everybody in The NSA lost, failed, and all villains who survived pleaded guilty. Everybody in the former Homeland Security lost, failed, and all villains who survived pleaded guilty. Everybody in the former FBI lost, failed, and all villains who survived pleaded guilty. All imposters,

impersonators, decoys, proxies, clones, and

gamblers who weren't using their bet to try

to help save an innocent, good or decent

person's life or welfare-- all lost, failed,

and all villains who survived pleaded guilty.

All Trumps lost, failed, and all villains who

survived pleaded guilty. All Clintons lost, failed,

and all villains who survived pleaded guilty.

All people who work for The Trumps lost, failed,

and all villains who survived pleaded guilty.

All people who work for The Clintons lost, failed,

and all villains who survived pleaded guilty.

All people who stole other peoples' identities

to try to hide their crimes behind them-- lost, failed,

and all villains who survived pleaded guilty.

All violators, assaulters, abusers, torturers,

tormenters, traitors, kidnappers, and exploiters

of innocent people or pets-- lost, failed,

and all villains who survived pleaded guilty.

All human traffickers lost. All 1st, 2nd, 3rd,

4th and 5th degree rapists-- which includes all

brain rapists and bioterrorists of the innocent--

lost, failed, and all villains who survived

pleaded guilty. All pedophiles, child molesters
and other sex offenders all lost, failed, and--
those who survived-- pleaded guilty.
All murderers of the innocent-- lost, failed,
and-- those who survived-- pleaded guilty.
All consciousness overriders lost, failed,
and all villains who survived pleaded guilty.
All chemical mind control inducers lost, failed,
and all villains who survived pleaded guilty.
All "Oculus Apocalypse" drug spreaders and
sellers lost, failed, and all villains who survived
pleaded guilty. All spies in disguise lost.
All "smoke and mirrors" hustle con
manipulators lost. All scam artists lost.
All perverse engineers lost.
All people who knowingly compel, direct,
order, carry out or otherwise facilitate pain,
damage, sickness, loss, oppression and/or
other violation against the innocent-- lost.
All orchestrators of assault, violence,
bioterrorism, abuse or other serious, intimate
or obscene violations against the innocent
and/or their basic human rights-- lost.
All directors of evil who do things like

arranging for innocent people to get

preyed upon, or blocking innocent people

from their wealth, success or freedom-- lost.

All people who knowingly wrongfully

imprison or trap innocent people-- lost.

All people who knowingly try to

control innocent people-- lost.

All people who knowingly try to place

fraudulent conservatorships over

innocent people against their will or

without their knowledge-- lost.

All people who otherwise knowingly

try to rob innocent people-- lost.

All people who try to block innocent people

from knowing the truth-- lost.

And all other supervillains and vicious

savage demon monsters-- lost,

cause all bad guys--

all enemies of the light--

all menaces to righteousness--

all threats against us-- all lost.

Everyone I've mentioned here lost, failed,

and all villains who survived-- pleaded guilty.

Awed Abraham starts to take a breath to speak, but Truth humorously cuts him off like a teenager with blinders on, to continue very matter-of-factly informing him…

TRUTH

And also all imposters, fraudulent

impersonators and spy aliases lost, failed

and all villains who survived pleaded guilty--

especially all presidential 1st family spy aliases,

including but not limited to all of the spies,

fraudulent impersonators or other imposters

using the aliases: George Washington, Martha

Washington, John Adams, Abigail Adams,

Thomas Jefferson, Aaron Burr, George

Clinton, James Madison, Dolley Madison,

Elbridge Gerry, James Monroe, Elizabeth

Kortright Monroe, Daniel D. Tompkins,

John Quincy Adams, Louisa Catherine

Adams, John C. Calhoun, Andrew Jackson,

Rachel Jackson, Martin Van Buren, Hannah

Hoes Van Buren, Richard M. Johnson,

William Henry Harrison, Anna Tuthill

Symmes Harrison, John Tyler, Letitia

Christian Tyler, Julia Gardiner Tyler,

James K. Polk, Sarah Childress Polk,

George M. Dallas, Zachary Taylor,

Margaret Mackall Smith Taylor, Millard

Fillmore, Abigail Powers Fillmore, Franklin

Pierce, Jane M. Pierce ,William R. King,
Franklin Pierce, Jane M. Pierce, James
Buchanan, John C. Breckinridge, Abraham
Lincoln, Mary Todd Lincoln, Hannibal Hamlin,
Andrew Johnson, Eliza McCardle Johnson,
Ulysses S. Grant, Julia Dent Grant, Schuyler
Colfax, Henry Wilson, Rutherford Birchard
Hayes, Lucy Webb Hayes, William A. Wheeler,
James A. Garfield, Lucretia Rudolph Garfield,
Chester A. Arthur, Ellen Lewis Herndon Arthur,
Grover Cleveland, Frances Folsom Cleveland,
Thomas A. Hendricks, Benjamin Harrison,
Caroline Lavinia Scott Harrison, Mary Lord
Harrison, Levi P. Morton, Adlai E. Stevenson,
William McKinley, Ida Saxton McKinley,
Garret A. Hobart, Theodore Roosevelt, Edith
Kermit Carow Roosevelt, Charles W.
Fairbanks, William H. Taft, Helen Herron
Taft, James S. Sherman, Woodrow Wilson,
Ellen Axson Wilson, Edith Bolling Galt
Wilson, Thomas R. Marshall, Warren G.
Harding, Florence Kling Harding, Calvin
Coolidge, Grace Goodhue Coolidge, Charles
G. Dawes, Herbert Hoover, Lou Henry Hoover,

Charles Curtis, Franklin D. Roosevelt, Eleanor

Roosevelt, John N. Garner, Henry A. Wallace,

Harry S. Truman, Bess Wallace Truman,

Alben W. Barkley, Dwight D. Eisenhower,

Mamie Doud Eisenhower, Richard M. Nixon,

John F. Kennedy, Jacqueline Kennedy, Lyndon

B. Johnson, Lady Bird Johnson, Hubert H.

Humphrey, Pat Nixon, Spiro T. Agnew, Gerald

R. Ford, Betty Ford, Nelson Rockefeller,

Jimmy Carter, Rosalynn Carter, Walter F.

Mondale, Ronald Reagan, Nancy Reagan,

George H.W. Bush, Barbara Bush, Dan

Quayle, Bill Clinton, Hillary Rodham Clinton,

Albert Gore, George W. Bush, Laura Bush,

Richard Cheney, Barack Obama, Michelle Obama,

Joseph R. Biden, Donald J. Trump, Melania Trump,

Mike Pence, Jill Biden Kamala Harris--

or any 1st or 2nd Family Children, Grandchildren,

Brothers, Sisters, Aunts, Uncles, or other 1st or 2nd

Family relatives-- who all lost, who all failed, and

of whom all villains who survived pleaded guilty.

Once again, Abraham starts to take a breath to speak, but Truth humorously cuts him off like a teenager with blinders on, to continue very matter-of-factly informing him…

TRUTH

And also all imposters, fraudulent

impersonators and spy aliases for all celebrities,

public figures, and private citizens or civilians,

including but not limited to fraudulent

impersonators of ourselves, our friends, our

family members, our neighbors, our classmates,

our co-workers, actors, movie stars, tv stars,

musicians, pop stars, titans of industry and etc--

and every villain and every villain's minions--

all those who aided and abetted the villains, or

who looked the other way when it was their job

to stop the villains-- as well as all the

Mysterio-From-Spiderman villains out there

who secretly cause problems just to pretend to

be the heroes fixing the very problems that

they themselves created-- all lost, failed

and all villains who survived pleaded guilty.

Abraham stares at Truth. She smiles innocently and bubbly at him. He's not sure if he should laugh or wait for secret instructions, as he opens his mouth sort of timidly to speak. Then Truth takes another breath-- and he stops-- and she looks the other way to cover her mouth as she SNEEZES with a funny little squeak.

ABRAHAM

God bless you.

TRUTH

Thank you-- You too.

ABRAHAM

Is… that all? Are you… done?

TRUTH

(nods thoughtfully)

I think so. Maybe. Probably.

ABRAHAM

(nods back, stunned)

Cool...Wow, Truth...That's-- a lot of stuff

we didn't cover in our little adventure

here. You even listed like 130 names.

TRUTH

(shrugs)

I learned a lot from Glinda while I was

but a ghost.

ABRAHAM

(chuckles with curiously

anxious surprise)

Yeah you did... So-- wait, then--

So nobody won?

TRUTH

So nobody won-- except for us--

The Good Samaritans. *We* won. ***And***

we're the only ones who won. See?

Truth shows Abe the new election results on her smartwatch, which displays 0 points for the leftwing, 0 points for the rightwing, and 0 points for the downwing, with 100% points for the upwing-- The Good Samaritans.

ABRAHAM

Oh cool!

TRUTH

And now we rule the house. ***AND*** I won,

earned, inherited, and received the

reparations I was owed in the amount of

$999 Billion Dollars. Glinda gave it to me.

(holds up shiny gold bank debit

card for Abe to see)

Dig it?

ABRAHAM

I'm diggin'it.

Abe nods cheerfully victoriously and gives Truth a cool-funny hi-5…

--An excerpt from "The Party: Welcome To Oz" @ http://tinyurl.com/ReadTheParty

~ <u>08</u> ~

~

<u>*DEAR RECRUITER: BAKER ACT THE WORLD*</u>
<u>*(BAKER ACT SONG)*</u>
<u>*Copyrighted © 2018 by Christi Luv AKA Chris*</u>
<u>*Taylor*</u>
<u>*(AKA "O'loveya Hail-Nope")*</u>

~

<u>*VERSES:*</u>
We can Baker Act bad boyfriends
And that girl he stalks, cause she won't go
on a date.
We can Baker Act bad bosses –
Or that employee who's always running late.

We can Baker Act your coworker –
So you can be promoted Winner out the

gate.
We can Baker Act rape victims –
As a vile way to retaliate.

We can Baker Act our landlords –
When we can't pay our rent on time.
We can Baker Act our tenants –
When we wanna sell & hike the rent sky
high.

We can Baker Act the police, the press –
Or anybody with a different point of view.
We can Baker Act our teachers, parents,
pastors.
& while we're at it-- LET'S BAKER ACT YOU
TOO!

CHORUS:
Let's Baker Act THE WORLD –
Whenever it doesn't go our way.
Let's Baker Act THE WORLD –
On a whim, on a lie – cause we had a bad
day.

Let's Baker Act THE WORLD –
Since you've let the innocent get violated
for a quota to fill.
Let's Baker Act THE WORLD –
If you'll lock ANYBODY up against their will.

HOOK:
JUST BAKE – BAKE – BAKE –
BAKER ACT 'EM
BAKE – BAKE – BAKE –
BAKER ACT 'EM
JUST BAKE – BAKE – BAKE –
BAKER ACT 'EM
YOU LET THEM HAVE CAKE
INSTEAD OF RIGHTS
WHEN YOU BAKER ACT 'EM

<u>*VERSES:*</u>
We can Baker Act our neighbors –
When they play their music too loud.
We can Baker Act homeowners –
So we can foreclose their homes to bidding
crowds.

We can Baker Act ex-spouses –
So we can get child custody 'n such.
And speaking of kids-- Let's Baker Act them
too –
Cause hey– They just talk back too much.

We can Baker Act all our enemies
To make them pay for what they've done to
us.
We can Baker Act all our friends –
If we're bored, if we're dumb 'n well-- JUST
CAUSE.

We can Baker Act the police, the press –
Or anybody with a different point of view.
We can Baker Act our teachers, parents,
pastors.
& while we're at it-- LET'S BAKER ACT YOU
TOO!

<u>*CHORUS:*</u>
Let's Baker Act THE WORLD –
Whenever it doesn't go our way.
Let's Baker Act THE WORLD –
On a whim, on a lie – cause we had a bad
day.

Let's Baker Act THE WORLD –
Since you've let the innocent get violated
for a quota to fill.
Let's Baker Act THE WORLD –
If you'll lock ANYBODY up against their will.

<u>*HOOK:*</u>

JUST BAKE – BAKE – BAKE –
BAKER ACT 'EM
BAKE – BAKE – BAKE –
BAKER ACT 'EM
JUST BAKE – BAKE – BAKE –
BAKER ACT 'EM
YOU LET THEM HAVE CAKE
INSTEAD OF RIGHTS
WHEN YOU BAKER ACT 'EM

BRIDGE:

We can Baker Act them billionaires –
To try to steal their honey.
We can Baker Act them patients there –
For their insurance money.

We can Baker Act them protesters
To shut 'em up 'n FREEZE 'em.
We can Baker Act them snitches there –
SO NO ONE WILL BELIEVE THEM.

We can Baker Act YOU Baby!
If I want you to talk more respectfully.
We can Baker Act YOU Baby!
If, well-- you just don't hook up with me.

We can Baker Act YOU Baby!
If I disagree with you politically.
We can Baker Act YOU Baby!
If, hey-- you shouldn'ta broke up with me.

We can Baker Act YOU Baby!
If I don't like the stuff you preach.
We can Baker Act YOU Baby!
If I hate that you never say HI to me.

We can Baker Act YOU Baby!
If I don't like your freedom of speech.
We can Baker Act YOU Baby!
If I just don't dig the way you look at me.

So let's Baker Act YOU Baby!
They'll tackle you half-naked in your room
tonight.
Yeah let's Baker Act YOU Baby!
And shove you in a cop car without reading
any rights.

Oh, let's Baker Act YOU Baby!
And strip-search you nude in cold
humiliation.
Now let's Baker Act YOU Baby!
And pump you with psychotic drugs in
LOUD deprivation.

So let's Baker Act YOU Baby!
With heroin junkies, HIV guys & piss on the
floor.
Yeah, let's Baker Act YOU Baby!
With girls, men & lesbians roomed together,
door-to-door.

Oh, let's Baker Act YOU Baby!
With screaming PSYCHOS & dudes
trash-diggin for food to eat.
Now, let's Baker Act YOU Baby!
With no access to fresh air and sunlight
until next week.

CLIMACTIC BREAK:
Let's Baker Act – Baker Act – Baker Act The
WORRRRRLLLLLDDDDD!!!!!

(CHEERFUL GROUP CHANT)
Why though? CAUSE WE _SAID_ SO!
IT'S HE-SAID/SHE-SAID BUT WHAT *I* SAID
GOES!

CHANNEL-VERSE REPRISE:
We can Baker Act the police, the press –
Or anybody with a different point of view.

We can Baker Act our teachers, parents,
pastors.
& while we're at it-- LET'S BAKER ACT YOU
TOO!

CHORUS: (X2)
Let's Baker Act THE WORLD –
Whenever it doesn't go our way.
Let's Baker Act THE WORLD –
On a whim, on a lie – cause we had a bad
day.

Let's Baker Act THE WORLD –
Since you've let the innocent get violated
for a quota to fill.
Let's Baker Act THE WORLD –
If you'll lock ANYBODY up against their will.

HOOK: (X2)
JUST BAKE – BAKE – BAKE –
BAKER ACT 'EM
BAKE – BAKE – BAKE –
BAKER ACT 'EM
JUST BAKE – BAKE – BAKE –
BAKER ACT 'EM
YOU LET THEM HAVE CAKE
INSTEAD OF RIGHTS
WHEN YOU BAKER ACT 'EM

AD-LIB COOL-SPEAK / CHANT COUNTERPOINT;
If you leave your rights
up to common sense,
You might be disappointed and let down.

Cause it's been a long time since
common sense was common
As misunderstood abuse of power sticks
around.

(CHEERFUL GROUP CHANT)

Why though? CAUSE WE _SAID_ SO!
IT'S HE-SAID/SHE-SAID BUT WHAT *I* SAID
<u>GOES!</u>

It's like The Purge in reverse –
So instead of criminally perverse,
Everyone's The Police, see –
But where's accountability?

It's like The Purge in reverse –
So instead of criminally perverse,
Everyone's The Police, see –
But where's accountability?

<u>(CHEERFUL GROUP CHANT)</u>
Why though? CAUSE WE _SAID_ SO!
IT'S HE-SAID/SHE-SAID BUT WHAT *I* SAID
<u>GOES!</u>

SO LEMME BAKER ACT **YOU** BABY!
CAUSE MAYBE **I'M** THE ONE WHO'S **CRAZY.**
SO I'MA BAKER ACT **YOU** BABY!
CAUSE MAYBE **I'M** THE ONE WHO'S <u>**CRAZY.**</u>

<u>(CHEERFUL GROUP CHANT)</u>
Why though? CAUSE WE _SAID_ SO!
IT'S HE-SAID/SHE-SAID BUT WHAT *I* SAID
<u>GOES!</u>

YEAH MAYBE **I'M** THE ONE WHO'S **CRAZY.**
BUT I BAKER ACTED **YOU** BABY!
YEAH MAYBE **I'M** THE ONE WHO'S **CRAZY.**
BUT I GOT **YOU** LOCKED UP BABY!

<u>(CHEERFUL GROUP CHANT)</u>
Why though? CAUSE WE _SAID_ SO!
IT'S HE-SAID/SHE-SAID BUT WHAT *I* SAID
<u>GOES!</u>

~ _13_ ~

~

Vacation
The Aftershow Special

~

O'loveya wakes up in the back of a limo after it stops abruptly. She looks up, confused.

O'loveya: What... What happened? Are the guys already at the resort?

The driver silently gets out, goes over to her side and opens her door... She looks up at him as he helps her out.

The Driver: Madam-- There is more to the story then you were actually told. Please follow me.

O'loveya: (confused) O...K...

O'loveya gets out of the limo and follows The Driver beyond the curb of The Tropical Beach Resort Hotel and into the lobby, towards the opposite end, out of the back glass doors, and into the big beautiful pool/jacuzzi area out back. He leads her to the tiki bar outdoor lounge where she sees the backs of a few guys sitting at the bar, talking and laughing. The Driver ushers for her to sit next to one of them, at the only bar stool left available, on the end. She stares at him quizzically. He almost begs her to just sit there, with his tiredly knowing, pleading expression, which she doesn't understand, as he looks tentatively around, almost like he's a defector from a cult, one who's not sure if his cult leader is gonna pop back up and nab him-- or kool aid him. She accommodates him and sits down, glancing to see if the bartender will catch a busy glimpse at her and take a drink order from her. He sees her and lifts his finger to signal that he's on his way to her. She nods. Then she hears a familiar voice-- though not one she's ever heard in person-- just on radio, TV, and movies.

The REAL Dustin: Hey girl-- Fancy meeting you here.

O'loveya: (looks at him and double-takes in confusion) Dustin? You look-- different. How'd you-- have time to change up your whole look in just-- like-- a few minutes? (sees the FBI badge hanging from a chain around his neck) And where'd you get that?

The REAL Dustin: (glances with a stifled chuckle at his badge) Oh this old thing? Just something I earned while working with some people to get you out of this insanity. (he discretely flips his badge around to inconspicuously show the NSA badge on the other side of it) And I haven't changed my look up in a while. I think you're confusing me with some clone-like impersonators from the deep state presidential fraternity. They've used impersonators to scam, manipulate, abuse, con, and take advantage of people-- to steal their trust. I'm The REAL Dustin. The guy you originally thought was me-- was not actually me-- not in the beginning. His real name is Jasper. Same for these guys-- (points at 3 other guys, 2 of whom look like the other guys from the contest) That's The REAL Trent-- not to be confused with his cloned impersonator, whose real name is JR.

The REAL Trent: Hello. (nods and waves shyly to O'loveya, who nods curiously at him)

The REAL Dustin: That's The REAL Clever-- not to be confused with his cloned impersonator, whose real name is Jake. (nods and waves hello shyly to O'loveya, who nods curiously at him)

The REAL Clever: Hey. (nods and waves coolly to O'loveya, who nods back at him)

The REAL Dustin: That's Dustin Cheesegood and Preggie-Lean Page --.

The REAL Dustin Cheesegood and Preggie-Lean Page: Hello. (pleasantly nod-waving slightly at O'loveya, who does the same back)

The REAL Dustin: And that's Allen-- He works for Homeland Security now.

The REAL Allen: Hi. (nods and waves preppy to O'loveya, who nods in awe at him)

O'loveya: Homeland Security?

The REAL Dustin: Yeah, O'loveya. I dunno if you noticed, but you're kinda the King Leader now. You have all the power. You have all the wealth. Now you need all the protection you didn't feel you were getting before-- and all the justice you need to further ensure that protection going forward. Both for yourself-- and for your allies-- or friends.

O'loveya: Power and wealth? You believe all that? I mean-- they're a cult.

The REAL Dustin: A once rich and powerful cult that you now own and dominate-- because not only did they all betray a kingmaker and violate their own laws to do so-- as well as all of ours-- but they all lost all their bets to you when they gambled on their own weakmindedness-- instead of on your strength of character, strength of will, and strength of mind. Originally, we were gonna come in sooner to save you, but when we realized how close you were to dominating everyone in the biggest, hardest, toughest fraternity cult we've ever had to fight the public oppression and contagious psychopathy of, we figured we'd just help you conquer them--

The REAL Trent: (huffs indignantly)
--VANQUISH them.

The REAL Allen: Delete the worst and tame
the sparable.

The REAL Clever: If there *are* any sparable...

The REAL Dustin: So here we are. Oh-- and
don't cash that check they gave you. It was
a scam to phish the funds out of your REAL
account--

The REAL Allen: --which you, O'loveya, are
actually in control of now, after I was
because I saw them trying to rob you and I
blocked them. That's partly why they tried
to lock us out of things-- cause we're more
loyal to you than we are to the fraternity--
and these frats haven't usually taken too
kindly to TRUE loyalty, goodness, and truth.
(he starts digging in his pocket for
something)

O'loveya: (confused) Check? What check?
They gave me a check for all this madness
and brutality?

The REAL Clever: (smirks) Yeah.
A-please-don't-kill-us check. (shakes his
head)

The REAL Dustin: It's in the mail. They
figured you'd be less likely to ask questions
and find out it was fraudulent if nobody
handed it to you and you just cashed it by
yourself at an account you didn't even
know you had-- just another way to try to
keep you broke and powerless-- to try to
block you from all your wealth and power
that they actually have no real legitimate

power over-- or any right to-- legal or otherwise. Lemme have your hand.

O'loveya hands Dustin her hand as he pulls out a scanner and a hard copy of a fingerprint. He gently takes her hand and presses her thumbprint onto the scanner. Then he takes a digital snapshot of the hard copied fingerprint and waits to see it and the image of O'loveya's newly scanned fingerprint merge together and match 100% on his smart device screen. He sighs in genuine relief at this, nods gratefully to himself, and nods at the envelope that's suddenly in O'loveya's hands.

The REAL Dustin: "You may now do the honors yourself, Miss O'loveya Nope--"

The REAL O'loveya holds up the envelope in her hands.

The REAL O'loveya: That's funny-- How did that get there?

The REAL Trent: Your wealth suddenly showed up in your hands because it's yours. It belongs to you-- so it only answers to you and arrives for you. No more struggling to make ends meet ever again. People and things working against you, your aims, your needs, your desires or your will... It's now over in the future.

The REAL O'loveya: Narly. (admiring the envelope like it's foreign alien DNA) Whoa-- New Wealth is mine-- and now visibly in my hands. Trippy.

The REAL Dustin: This is your REAL access to your REAL bank account of wealth, which will not bounce back on you or deplete any funds. These are your media exploitation compensations, your media immortalization compensations, your clinical trial violation compensations, your daily decoy proxy spotter/impersonator tester compensations, your forever-safety-concerned-now compensations, your 18 years of stolen adult-aged time you can't get back compensations, your property damage compensations, your sexual violation and assault reparations, your pain and suffering reparations, your loved ones lost reparations, your criminal body-cloning reparations, your criminal consciousness-cloning reparations, your kingmaker "Save The World" Fund-- in case you wanna save the world after they completely wrecked yours-- and everything else they owe you for-- all wrapped in one.

O'loveya: (opens the envelope to find a shiny new black Amex card) What's on it?

The REAL Dustin and The REAL Trenton and The REAL Allen: $999 Billion dollars--

The boys look at each other, realizing they spoke in sync... ;) --They laugh.

The REAL Dustin: Something like that.

She gawks at them. They chuckle.

O'loveya: Wow... Thanks.

The REAL Trent: Don't thank us-- thank yourself. You endured all their psychotic crap and couldn't find any recourse for help to save you from it until this year.

Musta been a real Nightmare On Live Stream. Sorry for all the things they took away from you-- especially the things that money can't buy or replace. I wouldn't wish this 36-year hell on my worst enemy.

O'loveya: 36? I thought it was 22 years...

The REAL Dustin: (nods) This started before you were born. You just became aware of it recently because more people entered your life to Secret Service you. And their adult-exploitation live stream of you started 22 years ago. But the child-exploitation live stream of you started long before then.

O'loveya: You got the Secret Service involved? Well-- how'd you all arrange all this without any POTUS help on the inside?

The REAL Allen: Because none of the people you've encountered are really presidents or presidential family members. They were all imposters PRETENDING to be presidents and presidential family members. They were working for the presidential fraternity through the NSA which is employed by the CIA who technologically funds The Deep State with high-tech sci-fi gear, which they used to violate and abuse the mess out of you-- as far as we know.

O'loveya: (awed and slightly speechless) ...W... Why?

The REAL Dustin: To get you to clean house for them-- to get rid of all their worst people-- and all the ones who got in their way-- while you were on the presidential path they chose for you, chain-whipped to their White House, as they tried to control and steal all your wealth along the way, probably bioterrorizing you whenever they felt like it and replacing you with a clone of yourself as soon as you got too RICHLY rebellious for them to control. "Poor You" they could handle. But "Wealthy You" is uncontainable. For all we know they could have even taken so long with you in this long overly drawn-out ordeal of repeatedly extended deadlines since 2009-- simply because they were trying to make 1 of your clones match you more perfectly-- both outwardly and inwardly-- so that they could try to replace you with her as soon as you got your key to your wealth. She's the clone of you who Mrs. Cloneton adopted and raised like a daughter-- after building her in a lab like a doll-- alongside the clone of your mother, so she could replace both you and your mother with them and control them completely in the White House-- and in your bank accounts. And it only takes a year and a half to clone a 40-year-old to the exact same visible age. That's why I had to check your fingerprint before handing you your card. Because they only wanted their homegrown clones who they've enslaved to their conservatorships and bioterror threats to have access to wealth and power-- so they could try to control it and steal it from them. And from their originals too-- like you and me and the rest of us sitting here at this bar right now. And clones don't even have to know they're being used that way. Many of them don't. So I had to be sure you weren't a clone of yourself-- by matching your NON-impersonatable fingerprint to the fingerprint we've been manually scanning

of you every time you go donate plasma--
for the past 4 years. We all have hidden
hard copy images of your fingerprint in a
variety of secret locations so that we can
digitally match it to the digital files and
new scans of your fingerprint, by
rephotographing our hard copies of your
original fingerprints into our high-tech
surveillance scanners and then
automatically comparing the old and new
fingerprints against each other-- all just to
verify that you are actually you-- and not
somebody's incestuously homegrown
slave-brained clone-bot.

O'loveya: (horrified but fascinated)
Weirdness...

The REAL Trent: But there are a few people
we can't yet name who made a *significant*
difference in all this.

The REAL Allen: (casually raising his
eyebrows to himself) I just *WISH* I knew what
that difference *was*.

The REAL Dustin: ANY WAY-- A liberal
family-- The Clonetons-- abused you,
tortured you, damaged you, violated you
and did everything they could to destroy
you-- even getting a conservative family--
The Trucks-- to also severely abuse you,
torture you, damage you, violate you, and
do everything they could to destroy you
too-- all so they could get you to dominate
one of their families-- just so your
immeasurable wealth could become the
wealth of their family name. Yes, you would
control them-- but they would still also
have close connections with the biggest
greatest amount of sole-owned wealth on

the face of the planet-- because of you. That's why they worked so hard to destroy your life-- to pump you like a golden goose. Then get owned by that golden goose-- but still pump you for wealth-- and then try to get you out of the way, as soon as you birthed a baby heir that they could then commandeer, control, brainwash and pump like their new golden goose, as they replaced you with a homegrown slave-brained clone of yourself-- who may have known nothing about you-- which is why some of your double agent bioterrorists added some weight to you-- to keep you looking obviously noticeably different from your clones, who are mostly basically like Skinny Sex Slave Barbie Dolls who do whatever they're told and, like most clones homegrown and owned by the wealthy and powerful elite-- are just now getting direct access and full control over their own money conservatorships that The Clonetons and The Trucks and people like them have held full control over, in order to further control grown adults like slaves-- until you set them free earlier today in a text message you sent out from the limo about freeing slaves of financial oppression and victims of fraudulent conservatorships.

O'loveya: (stares at him a beat) That's a lot.

The REAL Allen: Yeah. And still all people could think about has been polling a vote on which bad guy they think is the worst guy-- The Trucks or The Clonetons.

O'loveya: Well that part seems obvious? The Trucks are President Snow in The Hunger Games while The Clonetons are President

Coin in The Hunger Games. So the Trucks have evil individuals inside their nest who were easily baited into showing us all their worst demonry, but-- The Clonetons actually initiated this whole thing and have a whole demonically evil monster machine operation in place to carry on the wicked work and diseased legacy of their pathologically deceptive mode and poisonous ideology of existence-- _long after they're gone_. Whereas, the evil of The Trucks typically dies with them-- and stays dead-- other than the common problem that hurt people hurt people. I mean-- You got bad guy Trucks who'd punch you in the face until you submit. Then you got bad guy Clonetons who'd do the same, pretend the other guy did it, persuade everybody to believe that ish with extravagant long-game shadow puppeteering, and then teach their kids and grandkids to do the same-- like a never-ending vicious cycle-- and then plot to rape a girl on her birthday just to make her a single mom who's easier to control and replace because she kicked her big strong man-- her only real fighting "Ride or Die" witness-- and big billionaire bank account keyholder-- to the curb, mistakenly thinking he was the knowing culprit when he wasn't-- but led to believe it by those who wanted to replace him as the most important trustworthy confidant and keyholder of her wealth in her life-- err-- mine-- I mean. The Trucks, I've heard, victimized and exploited their own kids-- and killed innocents randomly, abruptly, and spontaneously-- like their elder men were all sort of out of control. The Clonetons, I've heard, never brought their demonry and killing of innocents home to their kids and grandkids, I've heard, with regard to physically violating them or pimping them out to be physically violated, or to be killed, or trying to frame them for murder, unlike The Trucks, who-- evidently-- have had no self-control-- like a house divided-- which, therefore, was always inevitably going to fall, because of their in-feeding on each other-- unlike The Clonetons, who've kept their self-control issues out of the house, like a raccoon in the trash heap. They were always the more pathologically criminally insidious system of operation.

The REAL Dustin: And now you own them all.

O'loveya: (stunned) Wow... But-- what about the ghost in the machine?

The REAL Dustin: Ghost?

O'loveya: Yeah. The puppetmaster who's been engineering all these demons and orchestrating all this chaos all this time. I wouldn't be surprised if none of us were familiar with their face, name, alias or identity. They seem to be the one manipulating the overarching narrative here-- having instantly brought out the worst in everyone.

The REAL Dustin: (curiously alerted now) Huh... Ya know you might be right about that... Well-- when I know, you'll know-- when you know, I'll know-- and when any of us know, all of us will know. How 'bout that?

The REAL O'loveya: (smiling) Sounds good. (then she rubs her head as she glances at the FBI badges hanging from the chains around Trent and Clever's necks too, next to their NSA badges, and the Homeland Security badge on Allen, next to his FBI and NSA badges, and she thinks) OK... So... Um... Now what?

The REAL Dustin: Now-- threats to your existence get managed securely-- and permanently.

The REAL Allen: Yeah-- like they all get shot out into outer space.

The REAL Trent: Better than they deserve.

The REAL Clever: Here here.

The REAL Dustin: Everyone who helped you gets promoted-- generously.

The REAL Clever: (smirks) If you can tell the difference between the REAL allies and all the phonies who are just coming in at the tail end in the 11th hour, pretending to be allies just to get on board to escape their sinking supervillain's ship of horrors like fleeing cockroaches into the sea, because they saw the writings on the wall and figured they'd rather conform with the living 'n the law-minded rather than rebel with the dead 'n the lawless.

The REAL Dustin: Your puppy dog Bella gets returned to you, all totally healthy, happy, fully groomed, and free of all fleas, mites, ticks, itches, rashes, allergies, nervous compulsions and whatever else those creepy leviathans were torturing her with (humorously hands her a peppy pretty poodle from out of nowhere, which makes her squeal and grin gleefully) and your real mom gets returned to you-- no more slave-brained clones with various villain decoys overriding their consciousness every day like a bus full of strangers (gestures a hand to her to introduce her REAL mom-- who's suddenly standing on the opposite side of O'loveya, smiling with tearful excitement and weary joy)

O'loveya: (glances at her and jolts, stunned with a gasp-- 1st one of warlike trepidation-- then, she notices how different her mom appears-- like the way she use to be, and she gasps again, only this time more tentatively, somber) Mom?

Her mom holds her arms out and they hug. O'loveya looks at Dustin.

O'loveya: They seriously CLONED my MOM? You were SERIOUS??!

The REAL Dustin: (nods solemnly) Homeland Security just rescued her from the creepy deep state cult-- after they commandeered her and tried to brainwash her. Then I set your real mom up with her own place to stay down the road. But-- yeah. This deep state cult did a lot of WTF stuff no one with a soul, sanity or respect for anyone's human rights would do. But now you're free of it. As free as you wanna be. In fact, YOU, my dear-- (puts a loving hand on her shoulder blade) get to do whatever you want-- living life to your heart's content-- with whoever you want to live it with-- whenever and however you want to live it-- including finally taking that vacation you been needing and wanting for so long now. Feel free to take it, bae. And rest easy knowing-- that we got your back.

O'loveya: (cheers excitedly) YAY!! *I'M ON VACATION!!!!!!* HAHA!!

The REAL Dustin Fallriver: And speaking of your back--we heard about all that remote control back pain they were giving you.

O'loveya: Using new-age tech to horse-whip me like an old-school slave.

The REAL Dustin: (visibly disturbed by it) Right--

O'loveya: And left.

The REAL Dustin: (nods) Trent.

Trent pulls out a big black briefcase, lays it on the bar counter, and flips it open to reveal a bunch of black sunglasses and devices that look like TV remote controls, except that each one has a big red button on it. Trent starts handing out 1 device and 1 pair of sunglasses to everyone in their group. When he hands O'loveya hers, he holds onto it for a fleeting moment, as she takes it, to focus her attention on him as everyone starts putting on their sunglasses. She looks at him curiously. He smiles at her, as he releases the device and sunglasses to her. She smiles back at him, with unexpected shyness, as she brings the device and sunglasses closer to her. Cheesegood and Preggie-Lean Page notice and watch Fallriver and Trent exchange tentatively tolerant looks of interpersonal knowingness at each other and Cheesegood and Preggie-Lean Page look forwardly downward, preparing to take sips of their drinks.

The REAL Preggie-Lean Page: This is gonna be interesting...

The REAL Dustin Cheesgood: Yup.

O'loveya's the last one to put on her sunglasses and start studying her remote control.

The REAL Trenton Gates: (now wearing his sunglasses too) And now we all finally and permanently rid the world of the hell machine-- the torture drone that's been facilitating all of the terrorizing, tormenting, violating, invading, and abusing of Miss O'loveya Nope and her loved ones-- including her pets-- and other innocent people-- for over 30 years. O'loveya-- everyone-- if you would all please look to the sky behind you.

Now looking like the men in black, everyone turns to look behind themselves, and they see a child-sized drone buzzing around nearby in the bright blue sky, with no one nearby beneath it.

The REAL Trent: Buttons out.

Everybody pulls out their remote control devices, fidgeting with them.

The REAL Trent: Ready--

Everybody suddenly stills their controllers, curiously.

The REAL Trent: Aim--

Everybody copies Trent in aiming their remote control devices at the hell machine torture drone.

The REAL Trent: And-- FIRE!!

Everybody slams down hard on their big red buttons and KABOOM!! The hell machine torture drone EXPLODES in midair, to a few startled gasps of people further away, who watch as the fiery red combustioned spectacle of abused technical parts falls like flaming debris to the beach sand. Everyone applauds the final end of this aspect of the nightmare with a humorous golf clap.

The REAL Trent: Good job, everybody. And O'loveya-- now there'll be no more pain, suffering, violation, invasion, abuse, torture, terrorism, harassment, hustle con deception, fraudulent manipulation, personal loss, damage, interference, delays, blockades, sabotage, ill will, malice, or even gross stressers like bugs, crap, odors, or anything else disgusting or offensive to the senses or in your personal space or face. You are now the healthiest, freest, and most excellent-feeling person on this or any planet-- and now that we've blown up the hell machine-- now we can show you how we turned on the heaven machine-- which can and has only been programmed to make you feel good 24/7-- and never vexed, stressed or otherwise unwell.

O'loveya gasps with delighted marvel at this, putting a hand to her heart as Trent hands her a smart device remote control that shows her all the wonderful ways her body and mind are being healed and made to feel good-- also putting the control over her own body back in her own hands. Fallriver nods, taking a swig of his drink before placing his glass back on the bar counter and pulling out his remote control device again.

The REAL Dustin Fallriver: Buttons out!

Everybody pulls their buttons out again.

The REAL Dustin Fallriver: Ready--

Everybody copies Fallriver in steadying their devices, not sure where to point them or why.

The REAL Dustin Fallriver: Aim--

Everybody looks around as they copy Fallriver, aiming their remotes at a blank blue sky.

The REAL Dustin Fallriver: FIRE!!

Everybody just pushes their buttons, not sure what they're pushing it for. Suddenly, a loud rumble sounds off at the Kennedy Space Center-like space station off into the distance, before a giant fleet of space shuttles all skyrocket into the ether, through the clouds, and towards outer space, with a massive billowing cloud of smoky fire charging from their jet propeller pipes below. Everybody looks on, curiously watching the show.

The REAL Allen: What's this?

The REAL Dustin Fallriver: All the assholes

going to outer space for a very long time now, for all the cruel crimes they did to O'loveya-- including their use of that hell machine torture drone we just blew up. Cause after all-- drones don't hurt people-- pilots do. And now they can't hurt O'loveya or anybody else on this planet ever again. And that fully ends the nightmare of bioterrorism abuse, creepy deranged fraud, and control freak violations, plaguing O'loveya and our society. Just like the 2021 movie-- It's Redemption Day.

The REAL Allen: I'll drink to that! (lifts glass, take a sip)

Others nod and sip in agreement. Then, out of the 999 space shuttles that keep launching into space, fleet after fleet-- 1 shakes and wobbles with various old pieces falling off.

The REAL Clever: That one looks a bit sketchy.

The REAL Dustin Fallriver: Yeah, that one has all the sex offenders and child predators on it. Their crimes drew them the short end of the stick.

The REAL Clever: Sucks to be them.

The REAL Dustin Fallriver: Indeed.

An eavesdropping stranger draws closer to them with his friends nearby, awaiting their drink order.

Stranger: Hey did you guys just slingshot a bunch of O'loveya Hail-Nope's vicious predators into outer space? Some of which have been oppressing the hell out of the rest of us for decades too?

The REAL Clever: (grinning gleefully from ear to ear) That we did.

Stranger: (awed grinning admiration) Oh hell yeah-- Hey guys! (shouting to all his friends while pointing at O'loveya's new crew) These guys just cleansed our planet of a bunch of demon-ruled savages and sent them all to outer space! Drinks on us!

The REAL Allen: (cheerful face lights up) Ah, *nice*--

Everybody applauds, cheers, whoops, whistles and hollers excitedly, some patting the guys' shoulders or giving hi-5's to Dustin Fallriver and O'loveya. Fallriver and some of the guys grin and chuckle. Then Dustin's eyes fall on O'loveya, and he pauses slightly, noticing a change in her. Unsure of her shift in demeanor, he tries to assure her of her new freedom and power.

The REAL Dustin Fallriver: Oh and don't worry. The NSA network is now yours-- if you want it-- or you can just walk away and have nothing more to do with any of it, O'loveya-- But if you do decide to stay or return, just know that everybody does whatever you wish or whatever they perceive that you want to happen-- and they will always be responsive, honest, clear, concise, coherent, decent, helpful, knowledgeable, fully "in the know", and purposefully good and loyal to you, your allies and every good or decent human being in the world. And it's not whatever you "SAY" or "BELIEVE" that comes true-- it's whatever you WANT or WISH that comes true-- which requires human intelligence to decipher-- not a dumb machine or a soulless algorithm. So now, if you want to-- you can go change the world. We can make it better-- as individuals a part-- or as a family-- together. Or you can just chill out. Whatever works for you.

For the 1st time, tears crescent O'loveya's sad, soulful, puppy dog eyes, and unable to repress it, she flings her arms out and embraces Dustin in a big, warm, cozy hug. Trent stretches his neck out.

The REAL Trent: Hey-- I want one of those!

Chuckling through the visible tears she sniffs back now, O'loveya fist bumps with a charmingly amused Trent, while still hugging Dustin Fallriver.

O'loveya: Thank God for you. All of you. Thank God for your existence.

The REAL Dustin Fallriver: (tenderly hugging her back with an irrepressible blush) Thank God you're completely safe and totally free now. (kisses her cheek sweetly)

O'loveya blushes, suddenly slightly shy-smiling at him. Then the bartender brings her a drink.

O'loveya: Oh, but I didn't order anything.

The Bartender: (nods at Dustin) He did.

O'loveya glances curiously at Dustin, who smiles playfully at her.

The REAL Dustin Fallriver: I know what you like, girl.

He winks charmingly at her with a twinkle in his pretty blue-eyed soul.

She giggles with him. Then he raises a glass.

The REAL Dustin Fallriver: To Truth!

Everybody: (raises a toast with him, clicking their glasses with his) To Truth! Here here!

They all sort of chuckle jovially and take a swig of their cocktails as O'loveya and Dustin smile curiously at each other...

The End... of The Nightmare.

The Beginning... of Paradise.

~ <u>FYI: For The Purpose of Clarity & Better Understanding</u> ~

<u>OUR ALIASES ARE AS FOLLOWS:</u>

O'LOVEYA HAIL-NOPE = ME

THE REAL DUSTIN FALLRIVER
OF *NSTED =
The original, non-impersonated, non-clone

JUSTIN TIMBERLAKE
OF *NSYNC
(impersonated by Jasper Bryce)

THE REAL TRENTON GATES
OF BRiDE =
The original, non-impersonated, non-clone
BRENTON THWAITES
OF SLiDE
(impersonated by J.R. Kirby)
NOTE: SLiDE is a show in which "Luke
Gallager" = J.R. Kirby--
not Justin Timberlake.

THE REAL CLEVER ZARK
OF COMEDY TV =
The original, non-impersonated,
non-clone TREVOR NOAH
OF THE DAILY SHOW
(impersonated by Jake Timberlake)

THE REAL ALLEN iBANG
OF FURY PLANTER =
The original, non-impersonated, non-clone
ALFRED ENOCH
OF HARRY POTTER

THE REAL DUSTIN CHEESEGOOD AND
OF JANGLE JINGLE =
The original, non-impersonated, non-clone
JUSTIN CORNWELL
OF JINGLE JANGLE

THE REAL PREGGIE-LEAN STAGE OF TREES
=
The original, non-impersonated, non-clone
REGE-JEAN PAGE OF ROOTS

In Virgins vs Aliens: Prom King
Sammy King = The FBI
& My Allies In The NSA/CIA/Deep State

Nick O'Brien = Homeland Security
& The Presidential Fraternity

Love Jones = My Freedom

DeVille = My Calculated / Psychopathic Enemies & Threats In The NSA/CIA/Deep State & Abroad (starting with Spy "Aliases" such as: Robert Trump, Jonathan Bailey, Donald Trump Sr and Hillary Clinton), As Well As Anyone Who Has Ever Knowingly Tried To 1st or 2nd Degree Rape or Destroy An Innocent Person (Including 'Innocent Persons' Like Me)

Holly's Brother Splinter = My Deranged / Sociopathic Enemies & Threats In The NSA/CIA/Deep State & Abroad (starting

with Spy "Aliases" such as: Donald Trump Jr,
Bill Clinton, Bill's Rapey Son Who I Call "Bill
Jr" & Reed Henrikson), As Well As Anyone
Who Has Ever Knowingly Tried To 1st or 2nd
Degree Rape or Destroy An Innocent Person
(Including 'Innocent Persons' Like Me)

Holly Wood = My Traitorous / Retarded
Enemies & Threats To My Existence,
Freedom or Rights (starting with all the
minions of my enemies and anyone who
facilitates threats to me) & Anyone Who Has
Ever Knowingly Facilitated Someone Else In
Trying To 1st, 2nd or 3rd Degree Rape,
Consciousness Override or Destroy An
Innocent Person (Including 'Innocent
Persons' Like Me)

_Only the guilty will be held accountable for
their crimes._
_No innocent and/or undeserving people
will ever be harmed, ended, or otherwise
hurt because of something I wrote, typed,
published or said._

~~~~~~
~~~~~~

_Read More @ TinyURL.com/ReadLuvKindles
~
or TinyURL.com/ReadLuvPaperbacks ~
And you can "Tip The Author" at
Paypal.me/ChristiLuvTV ~
Or TinyURL.com/SquareMonthly ~_

Fridays or email
HigherPowerPublishing@gmail.com for
sneak peeks.

To Indulge In An Amusing Fantasy Romance
Melodrama Read Virgins vs Aliens (13 book
series) Kindle Edition @
TinyURL.com/VirginsVsAliens or Get Real
with The Dear Recruiter Series @
TinyURL.com/DearHomelandSecurity - and
FYI: I am copyrighted © 1984 by The Creator
of The Universe-- & no one else.

~~~~~~
~~~~~~

*Sweet Jason is real to me ~ from Love
Me Tender
Pure Hunter is real to me ~ from
Hunting Love
Loyal Sammy King is real to me ~ from
Prom King
Loyal Nick O'Brien is real to me too,
just for fun*

*Noble Hero is real to me ~ from
Princess Wars
His Valiant Brothers, Plato & Romeo,
are real to me too
Courageous Comet is real to me ~ from
Angel Wars
Wise Abraham is real to me ~ from The
Party crew*

*Patient Joe is real to me ~ from Alien
Wars
Selfless Angel is real to me ~ from
Breathe
Dauntless Torch is real to me ~ from
Prophet Wars
Brilliant Skyler Stone is real to me ~
from truth I've seen*

*Though, I wish I was more patient, like
Melody
I wish I was more courageous, like siren*

Love Jones
I wish I was as FREED as Sammy's Love
becomes
I wish I had Sophia's shameless stones

I wish I was more focused, like Princess
I wish, like hers, my curse was also
lifted
I wish I was as powerful as Lady
Phantom
I wish I helped cure the world like Truth
did

I wish I was more disciplined, like Mary
I wish I had the ghostly blessing
Beauty had
I wish I felt a man love and fight for me
as Torch did Hope
I wish I was still in tune with
metaphysics, like Shyanne

I wish I could live in my imagination
I wish my good fiction worlds were
physically real
I wish I met a guy like my strong
passionate loving lead men
I wish I felt every high my lovely leading
ladies feel

I know the world will be a better place
when
My heroic characters come to life in
humanity
From my books, songs, and movies to
every youth they inspire
I won't stop till my fantasy's a reality

Cause the world is not as it should be

And everything you speak into
existence manifests
Every thought you think has a
vibration
Every act you make has a
consequence

So think the thoughts you want to
bring to life
Say the words you want to hear and
just--
Write the ideas you want to become
reality
<u>And live the way you wish the world
really was</u>

~ AMAZON.COM DESIRE GENRE GUIDE
~
Check out Christi Luv's published
works listed below with word count!
~
FOR THE LOVER IN YOU
A FANTASY THRILLER PASSION GUIDE
FOR THE ROMANCE LOVERS
~
~ THE CROWDED ROMANCE ~
INDULGE LOVE OR PICK A SIDE &
STAND BY YOUR LOVE LOYALLY
BY FACING LOVE TRIANGLES WITH
TORN PASSIONS
AND LOVE YOUR GOOD LOVE ~ EVEN
IN A PEACELESS PLACE
~
250K ~ Virgins vs Aliens: Season
1~"Prom King" (13 Screenplay-Novellas)
065K ~ Angel Wars: The Rise of Comet &
Lady Phantom (Novel 1)
045K ~ Shadow Wars: Young & Powerful
~ Gin's Escape (Screenplay 1)
035K ~ Shadow Wars Prequel: Virgins,
Vixens & Murder (Audioplay)
025K ~ Love Me Tender: The Existence
of Sound (Screenplay 1)
TBA-K~ Dear Recruiter: Scandal! (A
Series Within A Series)
~
~ THE FORBIDDEN ROMANCE ~
PROTECT LOVE & DEFEND YOUR LOVE
PROUDLY
BY FACING LOVE CHALLENGES WITH
DEFIANT PASSIONS
AND LOVE YOUR GOOD LOVE ~ EVEN
IN A FAITHLESS PLACE
~
80K ~ Siren Wars: Hunting Love & The

Blood Red Seductress (Novel 1)
45K ~ Alien Wars: The Perfect Child
(Screenplay 1)
30K ~ Princess Wars: Sleeping Beauty &
The Curse of Pirate Isle (Novella 1)
10K ~ Survival University: Jack In The
Box (Screenplay)
10K ~ ST&VT: Hottie Wars ~ Mr.
America's Cyborg Adventure
(Screenplay)
05K ~ Literary Rants: 1 Last Kiss For The
Runaway Boy (Short Story)

~

~ THE SAD ROMANCE ~
*RESCUE LOVE & GET YOUR LOVE
BACK VALIENTLY
BY FACING LOVE LOSSES WITH PINING
PASSIONS
AND LOVE YOUR GOOD LOVE ~ EVEN
IN A HOPELESS PLACE*

~

160K ~ The Killer Secrets of Skyler
Stone: My Funny Valentine (Novel 1)
065K ~ The Party: Welcome To Oz
(Screenplay 1)
055K ~ Prophet Wars: Mystic Eyes
(Screenplay 1)
010K ~ Survival University: Angel DeVille
(Screenplay)
010K ~ Literary Rants of A 13 Yr. Old Kid:
Unfinished Business (Play)
005K ~ Literary Rants of A 13 Yr. Old Kid:
Cyclone's House (Short Story)

~

~ THE BAD ROMANCE ~
*TEACH LOVE & LEARN WHAT LOVE IS
NOT
BY FACING LOVE FAILS WITH
BETRAYED PASSIONS*

~

15K ~ Dear Recruiter: My CRAZY Big
Brother! (Novelette)
10K ~ Sex, Truth & Videotape: Will Power
(Screenplay)
10K ~ Sex, Truth & Videotape: The
Rumor Mill (Screenplay)
10K ~ Sex, Truth & Videotape: Happy
Anniversary, Dr. Apocalypse! (Play)
10K ~ Sex, Truth & Videotape: The Diary
of Christi Luv ~ There's That Hair! (AKA
Dear Recruiter: My 1st BF Was A
Sociopath) (Prose)

~

~ *NO ROMANCE* ~

~

10K ~ Survival University: KiLL Club
(Novelette)
10K ~ Dear Recruiter: The
Superhero-Rape Experiment
(Novelette)
10K ~ Survival University:
3Shorts~HuntBros/SoulSavers/HopeH
eroes (Plays)
10K ~ Survival University: TDoCL ~
iBreathe, Therefore iWrite (Prose)

~

~ *TO BE ANNOUNCED* ~

~

TBA ~ Superhero Wars: The Crossover

Games (Novel)
TBA ~ Zombie Wars: *NSYNC SAVES
THE WORLD! (Screenplay)
TBA ~ Pop Star Wars: *NSYNC vs BSB ~
Boy Band Battle (Screenplay)
TBA ~ Supervillains In Love: The
Musical (Screenplay)
TBA ~ Breathe. (Novel)
~

*If you can't find a title request it at
HigherPowerPublishing@Gmail.com.*

~

***FOR THE FIGHTER IN YOU
A FANTASY THRILLER PASSION GUIDE
FOR THE BATTLE LOVERS***
~

~ THE CURSED FANTASY BATTLE ~
***FIND A CURE & BREAK THE CYCLE
BY FIGHTING TO HEAL WITH
PASSIONATE FAITH
AND FIGHT THE GOOD FIGHT ~ IN A
BROKEN PLACE***
~

80K ~ Siren Wars: Hunting Love & The Blood Red Seductress (Novel 1)
30K ~ Princess Wars: Sleeping Beauty & The Curse of Pirate Isle (Novella 1)
25K ~ Love Me Tender: The Existence of Sound (Screenplay 1)
15K ~ The Diary of Christi Luv: Dear Recruiter Letters of Poetry, Prose & Song
10K ~ Survival University: Angel DeVille (Screenplay)
10K ~ Sex, Truth & Videotape: Will Power (Screenplay)
05K ~ Literary Rants of A 13 Yr. Old Kid: Cyclone's House (Short Story)
TBA ~ Breathe. (Novel)
~

~ THE TRAPPED ADVENTURE BATTLE ~
***FIND FREEDOM & GET OUT
BY FIGHTING TO ESCAPE WITH
PASSIONATE HOPE
AND FIGHT THE GOOD FIGHT ~ IN A
BLOCKED PLACE***

~
65K ~ The Party: Welcome To Oz
(Screenplay 1)
55K ~ Prophet Wars: Mystic Eyes
(Screenplay 1)
45K ~ Shadow Wars: Young & Powerful ~
Gin's Escape (Screenplay 1)
15K ~ Dear Recruiter: My CRAZY Big
Brother! (Novelette)
10K ~ Survival University: Jack In The
Box (Screenplay)
10K ~ Sex, Truth & Videotape: The
Rumor Mill (Screenplay)
TBA ~ Zombie Wars: *NSYNC SAVES
THE WORLD! (Screenplay)
~

~ THE PUZZLED MYSTERY BATTLE ~
FIND THE TRUTH & SOLVE THE
BEFUDDLEMENT
BY FIGHTING TO DISCOVER WITH
PASSIONATE CURIOSITY
AND FIGHT THE GOOD FIGHT ~ IN A
TRICKED PLACE

~
160K ~ The Killer Secrets of Skyler
Stone: My Funny Valentine (Novel 1)
065K ~ Angel Wars: The Rise of Comet &
Lady Phantom (Novel 1)
010K ~ Literary Rants of A 13 Yr. Old Kid:
Unfinished Business (Play)
010K ~ Survival University: KiLL Club
(Novelette)
010K ~ Sex, Truth & Videotape: Happy
Anniversary, Dr. Apocalypse! (Play)
010K ~ Dear Recruiter: The
Superhero-Rape Experiment
(Novelette)
*TBA ~ Superhero Wars: The Crossover
Games (Novel)
~

*~ <u>**THE INVADED ROMANCE BATTLE**</u> ~*
<u>FIND A LIFELINE & GET THRU THE</u>
<u>PERIL</u>
<u>BY FIGHTING TO SURVIVE WITH</u>
<u>PASSIONATE LOVE</u>
<u>AND FIGHT THE GOOD FIGHT ~ IN AN</u>
<u>ATTACKED PLACE</u>
~

250K ~ Virgins vs Aliens: Season 1 ~
"Prom King" (13 Screenplay-Novellas)
045K ~ Alien Wars: The Perfect Child
(Screenplay 1)
035K ~ Shadow Wars Prequel: Virgins,
Vixens & Murder (Audioplay)
010K ~ ST&VT: Hottie Wars ~ Mr.
America's Cyborg Adventure
(Screenplay)
010K ~ Survival University:
3Shorts~HuntBros/SoulSavers/HopeH
ero (Plays)
005K ~ Literary Rants: 1 Last Kiss For
The Runaway Boy (Short Story)
*TBA ~ Pop Star Wars: *NSYNC vs BSB ~
Boy Band Battle (Screenplay)
*TBA ~ Supervillains In Love: The
Musical (Screenplay)
~

*~ <u>**THE AWAKENED NON-FICTION**</u>*
*<u>**BATTLE**</u> ~*
<u>FIND THE WISDOM & LEARN THE</u>
<u>LESSON</u>
<u>BY FIGHTING TO UNDERSTAND WITH</u>
<u>PASSIONATE INSIGHT</u>
<u>AND FIGHT THE GOOD FIGHT ~ IN A</u>
<u>CONNECTED PLACE</u>
~

10K ~ Dear Recruiter: TDoCL ~ My 1st BF
Was A Sociopath (Prose)
10K ~ Sex, Truth & Videotape: TDoCL ~

There's That Hair! (Prose)
10K ~ Survival University: TDoCL ~
iBreathe, Therefore iWrite (Prose)
60K ~ The Diary of Christi Luv: A
Love/Life Poetry Collection (Rhyme)
~

_**If you can't find a title request it at
HigherPowerPublishing@Gmail.com.**_

~ THE DIARY OF CHRISTI LUV:
POETRY/SONG ~ LIST OF EPISODES ~

~

*10K ~ The Diary of Christi Luv: Letters
of Poetry & Song ~ Dear Youth Life
10K ~ The Diary of Christi Luv: Letters
of Poetry & Song ~ Dear Faith Life
10K ~ The Diary of Christi Luv: Letters
of Poetry & Song ~ Dear Political Life
10K ~ The Diary of Christi Luv: Letters
of Poetry & Song ~ Dear Bad Love
10K ~ The Diary of Christi Luv: Letters
of Poetry & Song ~ Dear Puppy Love
10K ~ The Diary of Christi Luv: Letters
of Poetry & Song ~ Dear Forever Love
30K ~ The Diary of Christi Luv: Letters
of Poetry & Song ~ Dear Life Songs
30K ~ The Diary of Christi Luv: Letters
of Poetry & Song ~ Dear Love Songs
15K ~ The Diary of Christi Luv: Dear
Recruiter Letters of Poetry, Prose &
Song*

~ VIRGINS VS ALIENS ~ S1: "PROM KING"
~ LIST OF EPISODES ~

~

**40K ~ Season 01: Episode 01 ~ Wait For
Me, My Love
*20K ~ Season 01: Episode 02 ~ The
Virgin Love Triangle
*20K ~ Season 01: Episode 03 ~ Saving
Love
*20K ~ Season 01: Episode 04 ~ A Love
So Selfless*

*20K ~ Season 01: Episode 05 ~ Seduced
By Love
*20K ~ Season 01: Episode 06 ~ Love
Seduced By Sammy
*20K ~ Season 01: Episode 07 ~ The
Virgin Love Wedding
*20K ~ Season 01: Episode 08 ~ Love
Seduced By Nick
*20K ~ Season 01: Episode 09 ~ Virgin
Love & War
*20K ~ Season 01: Episode 10 ~ Virgin
Love Secrets
*25K ~ Season 01: Episode 11 ~ Prom
Night Love
*20K ~ Season 01: Episode 12 ~
Perverting Love
*30K ~ Season 01: Episode 13 ~ Love's
Song
250K ~ TOTAL COMPLETE S01 ~ "Prom
King"

~ VvsA (CONDENSED) ~ S1: "PROM KING" ~ LIST OF EPISODES ~

~

55K ~ Book 1 (Ep 1-2: Wait For Me, My
Love & The Virgin Love Triangle)
55K ~ Book 2 (Ep 3-5: Saving Love, A
Love So Selfless & Seduced By Love)
45K ~ Book 3 (Ep 6-8: Seduced By Sam,
Virgin Love Wed & Seduced By Nick)
50K ~ Book 4 (Ep 9-11: VirginLove/War,
VirginLoveSecrets & PromNightLove)
40K ~ Book 5 (Ep 12-13: Perverting Love
& Love's Song)

~ DEAR RECRUITER SERIES ~ LIST OF EPISODES ~

~

15K ~ CURSED: TDoCL ~ D.R. Letters of Poetry, Prose & Song
15K ~ TRAPPED: My CRAZY Big Brother! (Novelette)
10K ~ PUZZLED: The Superhero-Rape Experiment (Novelette)
TBA ~ INVADED: SCANDAL! (a series within a series)
10K ~ AWAKENED: TDoCL ~ My 1st BF Was A Sociopath (Prose)

~ *SEX, TRUTH & VIDEOTAPE SERIES ~ LIST OF EPISODES ~*

~

10K ~ CURSED: Will Power (Screenplay)
10K ~ TRAPPED: The Rumor Mill (Screenplay)
10K ~ PUZZLED: Happy Anniversary, Dr. Apocalypse! (Play)
10K ~ INVADED: Hottie Wars: Mr. America's Cyborg Adventure (Screenplay)
10K ~ AWAKENED: TDoCL ~ There's That Hair! (Prose)

~ *SURVIVAL UNIVERSITY SERIES ~ LIST OF EPISODES ~*

~

10K ~ CURSED: Angel DeVille (Screenplay)
10K ~ TRAPPED: Jack In The Box (Screenplay)
10K ~ PUZZLED: KiLL Club (Novelette)
10K ~ INVADED: 3 Shorts (Hunt Bros / Soul Savers / Hope Heroes) (Plays)
10K ~ AWAKENED: TDoCL ~ iBreathe, Therefore iWrite (Prose)

~ _LITERARY RANTS SERIES ~ LIST OF EPISODES_ ~

~

05K ~ CURSED: Cyclone's House (Short Story)
10K ~ PUZZLED: Unfinished Business (Play)
05K ~ INVADED: 1 Last Kiss For The Runaway Boy (Short Story)

~ _PIECES OF A MEMOIR SERIES ~ LIST OF EPISODES_ ~

~

10K ~ My 1st BF Was A Sociopath (Prose)
10K ~ iBreathe, Therefore iWrite (Prose)

~ _COMING SOON_ ~

~

90K ~ MIX: Christi Luv's Mega Collection of Short Stories & Novelettes
TBA ~ MIX: Christi Luv's Mega Collection Series of Long Fiction Samplers
TBA ~ AWAKENED: Luv's Hi5iQ Guide ~ 2Ur Natural Strengths
TBA ~ AWAKENED: Luv's Hi5iQ Guide ~ 2Ur Astro-Angel Strength
TBA ~ AWAKENED: Luv's Hi5iQ Guide ~ 2Ur Secret Strengths
TBA ~ AWAKENED: How 2 Write ~ Hit Songs w/Examples
TBA ~ AWAKENED: How 2 Write ~ Hit Movies w/Examples
TBA ~ AWAKENED: How 2 Write ~ Hit Books w/Examples
TBA ~ AWAKENED: *HERO Is The New BLACK! ~ Inventors

*TBA ~ AWAKENED: *HERO Is The New BLACK! ~ Pioneers*

*TBA ~ AWAKENED: *HERO Is The New BLACK! ~ Royalty (A Did You Know? Well You Should! Collection of Positive Black History Contributions Series)*

*TBA ~ AWAKENED: *Protecting Our Youth ~ Kids Rape Kids: How To Teach Your Children About Sex Before A Predator Does*

10K ~ AWAKENED: Philosophies Explained ~ Logic of Cursed Books

10K ~ AWAKENED: Philosophies Explained ~ Logic of Trapped Books

10K ~ AWAKENED: Philosophies Explained ~ Logic of Puzzled Books

10K ~ AWAKENED: Philosophies Explained ~ Logic of Invaded Books

10K ~ AWAKENED: Philosophies Explained ~ Logic of Awakened Books

50K ~ AWAKENED: Philosophies Explained ~ Logic of All Luv Books

<u>*~ AMAZON.COM THEME GUIDE ~*</u>
<u>*This list of Christi Luv's published*</u>
<u>*themes is subject to change/grow.*</u>
~
<u>*~ THE 10 COLLECTIONS OF LUV ~*</u>
~

<u>*THE ALIEN COLLECTION:*</u>
~ for "Why is this happening to me?"
chills & TRUTH fantasy thrills! ~

<u>*THE SEDUCTRESS COLLECTION:*</u>
~ for "Is he for real?" chills & ROMANCE
fantasy thrills! ~

<u>*THE KILLER COLLECTION:*</u>
~ for "Whodunit?" chills & REVENGE
fantasy thrills! ~

<u>*THE MAD-HATTER COLLECTION:*</u>
~ for "WTF?" chills & ESCAPE fantasy
thrills! ~

<u>*THE ADVENTURER COLLECTION:*</u>
~ for "What happens next?" chills &
ROLLER-COASTER fantasy thrills! ~

<u>*THE STUDENT COLLECTION:*</u>
~ for "Will they find out?" chills &
VICTORY fantasy thrills! ~

<u>*THE ANGEL COLLECTION:*</u>
~ for "How do we fulfill the prophecy?"
chills & MAGIC fantasy thrills! ~

<u>*THE SUPERHERO COLLECTION:*</u>
~ for "How do we stop the bad guys?"
chills & BATTLE fantasy thrills! ~

**THE CHARMER COLLECTION:**
~ for "How sweet is that?" chills &
FASCINATION fantasy thrills! ~

**THE ROCK STAR COLLECTION:**
~ for "When do we rock the stage?"
chills & PARTY fantasy thrills! ~

~
**~ THE ALIEN COLLECTION INCLUDES**
~
Virgins vs Aliens: Complete Season 1 ~
Prom King / E1-13 ~ (250K)
The Diary of Christi Luv: Poetry &
Songs ~ All Poems (60K)
Alien Wars: The Perfect Child (45K)
Survival University: TDoCL/P.O.A.M: I
Breathe, Therefore I Write (10K)
Sex, Truth & Videotape: Hottie Wars ~ A
Cyborg Adventure (10K)
~
**~ THE SEDUCTRESS COLLECTION**
**INCLUDES ~**
Siren Wars: Hunting Love & The Curse
of The Blood Red Seductress (80K)
Virgins vs Aliens ~ S1: "Prom King"
(Condensed) ~ 1/5 (55K)
Virgins vs Aliens ~ S1: "Prom King"
(Condensed) ~ 2/5 (50K)
Virgins vs Aliens ~ S1: "Prom King"
(Condensed) ~ 3/5 (45K)
Virgins vs Aliens ~ S1: "Prom King"
(Condensed) ~ 4/5 (50K)
Virgins vs Aliens ~ S1: "Prom King"
(Condensed) ~ 5/5 (40K)
Sex, Truth & Videotape: The Full Shorts
& Novelettes Collection (35K)
Sex, Truth & Videotape: Will Power (10K)
The Diary of Christi Luv: Poetry &

Songs ~ Bad Love (10K)
Sex, Truth & Videotape: TDoCL/POA
Memoir ~ There's That Hair! (10K)
~
~ *THE KILLER COLLECTION INCLUDES*
~
The Killer Secrets of Skyler Stone: My
Funny Valentine (160K)
Survival University: KiLL Club (10K)
Literary Rants of A 13 Year Old Kid:
Cyclone's House (5K)
Protecting Our Youth: Kids Rape Kids
(TBA)
~
~ *THE MAD-HATTER COLLECTION INCLUDES ~*
The Party: Welcome To Oz (65K)
Dear Recruiter: The Full Shorts &
Novelettes Collection (30K)
Dear Recruiter: My CRAZY Big Brother!
(15K)
Dear Recruiter: TDoCL/P.O.A.M. ~ My 1st
BF Was A Sociopath (10K)
The Diary of Christi Luv: Poetry &
Songs ~ Political Life (10K)
Sex, Truth & Videotape: Happy
Anniversary, Dr. Apocalypse! (10K)
~
~ *THE ADVENTURER COLLECTION INCLUDES ~*
Luv's Mega Collection of Short Stories
& Novelettes (90K)
Princess Wars: Sleeping Beauty & The
Curse of Pirate Island (30K)
The Diary of Christi Luv: Poetry &
Songs ~ Forever Love (10K)
Literary Rants of A 13 Yr Old Kid: 1 Last
Kiss For The Runaway Boy (5K)
Cursed/Trapped/Puzzled/Invaded/Awa
kened Genre Samplers (TBA)

~
~ *THE STUDENT COLLECTION INCLUDES* ~

Prophet Wars: Mystic Eyes (55K)
Survival University: The Full Shorts &
Novelettes Collection (40K)
The Diary of Christi Luv: Poetry &
Songs ~ Youth Life (10K)
Survival University: Jack In The Box
(10K)
Sex, Truth & Videotape: The Rumor Mill
(10K)
How 2 Write: Hit Movies w/Examples
(TBA)
How 2 Write: Hit Books w/Examples
(TBA)

~

~ *THE ANGEL COLLECTION INCLUDES*

~

Angel Wars: The Rise of Comet & Lady
Phantom (65K)
Survival University: Angel DeVille (10K)
The Diary of Christi Luv: Poetry &
Songs ~ Faith Life (10K)
Literary Rants of A 13 Year Old Kid:
Unfinished Business (10K)
Breathe. (TBA)
Luv's Hi5iQ Guide: 2Ur Astro-Angel
Strengths (TBA)
Luv's Hi5iQ Guide: 2Ur Natural
Strengths (TBA)
Luv's Hi5iQ Guide: 2Ur Secret
Strengths (TBA)

~

~ *THE SUPERHERO COLLECTION INCLUDES* ~

Shadow Wars: The Young & The
Powerful ~ Gin's Escape (45K)
The Diary of Christi Luv: Poetry &
Songs ~ Life Songs (30K)

Dear Recruiter: The Superhero-Rape
Experiment (10K)
Survival University: 3 Shorts ~ Hunt
Bros / Soul Savers / Hope Heroes (10K)
Zombie Wars: *NSYNC SAVES THE
WORLD! (TBA)
Superhero Wars: The Crossover Games
(TBA)
HERO Is The New BLACK! ~ Inventors
(TBA)
HERO Is The New BLACK! ~ Pioneers
(TBA)
HERO Is The New BLACK! ~ Royalty
(TBA)
~

~ THE CHARMER COLLECTION INCLUDES ~

Luv's Mega Collection of Long Fiction
Samplers (165K)
Philosophies Explained: The Logic of
All Luv Books (55K)
Love Me Tender: The Existence of
Sound (25K)
Literary Rants of A 13 Year Old Kid:
Total Collection (25K)
The Diary of Christi Luv: Poetry &
Songs ~ Puppy Love (10K)
Philosophies Explained: The Logic of
Cursed Books (10K)
Philosophies Explained: The Logic of
Trapped Books (10K)
Philosophies Explained: The Logic of
Puzzled Books (10K)
Philosophies Explained: The Logic of
Invaded Books (10K)
Philosophies Explained: The Logic of
Awakened Books (10K)
~

~ THE ROCK STAR COLLECTION INCLUDES ~

The Young & Powerful/SW Prequel ~
Real Talk: Virgins, Vixens & Murder
(35K)
The Diary of Christi Luv: Poetry &
Songs ~ Love Songs (10K)
Pop Star Wars: *NSYNC vs BSB ~ Battle
of The Boy Bands (TBA)
Supervillains In Love: The Musical
(TBA)
How 2 Write: Hit Songs w/Examples
(TBA)
~

*If you can't find a title, request it at
HigherPowerPublishing@Gmail.com.*
~
~ ***STAY UPDATED*** ~
*Follow The Author @
amazon.com/author/christiluv
Subscribe 4 Freebies @
christiluvtv.wix.com/VIPclub
Order A Book Subscription @
Patreon.com/AmazonBookClub
Donate To Author Projects @
Patreon.com/ChristiLuvTV
Tip The Author Just Because @
PayPal.com/ChristiLuvTV
or Venmo.com/ChristiLuvTV or easiest
@ TinyURL.com/SquareMonthly*
~
*Thank you for reading this book. Hope
you enjoyed the journey!*
***God Bless-- and see you soon, on the
next one!***
~

~ *AMAZON.COM ADULT MATURITY GUIDE* ~

TBD = To Be Determined
MHI = Mentioned, Hinted or Implied
Most Language = YA-safe {PG-13}
LPG = Language MG-appropriate {PG}

KISS = MG-(Mid-Grade/Kid)-Safe
Hetero Affection (Crush's Sweet Peck)
TOUCH = YA-(Young-Adult/Teen)-OK
Hetero Affection (Like Making Out)
SEX =
NA-(New-Adult/AFTER-High-School)-Re
stricted Hetero Affection
(Sodomy / deviant sex is rarely implied
or depicted & not encouraged)
RAPE = Sexual Violence / Spiritually
Intimate Robbery

NRV = Non-sexual "Real" (Reality)
Violence
NFV = Non-sexual "Fake" (Fantasy)
Violence
DRINK = Recreational Use of Alcohol
DRUG = Recreational Use of Nicotine
or Narcotics

BOOK:::::: KISS/TOUCH ~ SEX-/-RAPE ~ NRV/NFV ~ DRINK/DRUG

3ShortStories: No/No ~~~~ No/Yes ~~~~
Yes/Yes ~~~~~~MHI/No
**Alien Wars 1:* Yes/Yes ~~ Marital/Repro
~ Yes/Yes ~~~~~ Mom/No
Angel DeVille: Yes/No ~~~~ MHI/No ~~~~
Meh/Yes ~~~~~MHI/No
Angel Wars 1: Yes/No ~~~~ No/No ~~~~~
No/Yes ~~~ No/No/LPG
DearRecruiter: No/No ~~~~ MHI/Yes
~~~~Yes/Yes ~~~~~~ No/No
~~~~

DrApocalypse: Yes/Yes ~~~ Marital/No
~~~No/No ~~~~~~~No/No
**Hottie Wars:* No/No ~~~~ MHI/No ~~~~
No/Yes ~~~~~~~No/No
***Jack In Box:* No/No ~~~~ No/No ~~~~~
No/No ~~~~~~ MHI/No
*****KiLL Club:* No/No ~~~~ MHI/Yes
~~~~Yes/No ~~~~~~ No/No
Lit Rants/Kid: Yes/No ~~~~No/No ~~~~
Yes/Yes ~~~~ No/No/LPG
LoveMeTendr: Yes/Yes ~~~~No/No ~~~~
Yes/Meh ~~~~ Once/No
PrincessWar1: Yes/Yes ~~~~No/No ~~~~
Yes/Yes ~~~~ Pirates/No
ProphetWars1: Yes/No ~~~~No/No ~~~~
No/Yes ~~~~ No/No/LPG
SexTruthVido: Yes/Yes ~
Marital/Attempt ~ Yes/Yes ~~~~~~
No/No
ShadowWars1: Yes/Yes ~~ Yes/Attempt
~~ Yes/No ~~~~~~ No/No
SH-R Exprimnt: No/MHI ~~~ No/MHI
~~~~ MHI/No ~~~~~~ No/No
Siren Wars 1: Yes/Yes ~~ MHI/Attempt
~~ Yes/Yes ~~~~~~ No/No
SkylerStone 1: Yes/Yes ~~~ MHI/Yes ~~~~
Yes/No ~~~No/Rejected
SurvivalUnivrs: No/No ~~~~ MHI/Yes ~~~
Yes/Yes ~~~~~~MHI/No
**Y&P Prequel:* Yes/Yes ~~~~Yes/No ~~~
Yes/No ~~~~~~ Yes/No
The Party / Oz: Yes/Yes ~~~~MHI/No ~~~
Meh/Yes ~~~No/PopField
The RumorMill: No/No ~~~ No/Attempt
~~ Yes/No ~~~~~~~No/No
VirginsVsAlien: Yes/Yes ~~ MHI/Attempt
~~ Yes/Yes ~~~~~ Yes/No
****Will Power:* Yes/Meh ~~~ MHI/No ~~~~
~~~~

No/No ~~~~~~ No/No

NOVELS & MOVIE-LENGTH PLAYS (WORKS OVER 40K WORDS & PRESUMABLY OVER 90 MINUTES IN ADAPTED SCREEN TIME):

165K ~ Luv's Mega Collection of Long Fiction Samplers (Prose & Plays)
160K ~ The Killer Secrets of Skyler Stone: My Funny Valentine (Prose)
*90K ~ Luv's Mega Collection of Short Stories & Novelettes (P&P)
*80K ~ Siren Wars: Hunting Love / Blood Red Seductress Curse (Prose)
*65K ~ The Party: Welcome To Oz (Screenplay)
*65K ~ Angel Wars: The Rise of Comet & Lady Phantom (Prose)
*60K ~ Philosophies Explained: The Logic of All Christi Luv Books (Mix)
*60K ~ The Diary of Christi Luv: Poetry & Song ~ All Poems (Rhyme)
*55K ~ Prophet Wars: Mystic Eyes (Screenplay)
*55K ~ Virgins vs Aliens: Prom King ~ Condensed (Screenplays) 1/5
*50K ~ Virgins vs Aliens: Prom King ~ Condensed (Screenplays) 2/5
*50K ~ Virgins vs Aliens: Prom King ~ Condensed (Screenplays) 4/5
*45K ~ Shadow Wars: Young & Powerful ~ Gin's Escape (Screenplay)
*45K ~ Virgins vs Aliens: Prom King ~ Condensed (Screenplays) 3/5
*45K ~ Alien Wars: The Perfect Child

(Screenplay)
*40K ~ Virgins vs Aliens: Prom King ~
Condensed (Screenplays) 5/5

NOVELLAS & TV-LENGTH PLAYS (WORKS 17K – 40K WORDS & PRESUMABLY 60 TO 90 MINUTES IN ADAPTED SCREEN TIME):

250K ~ Virgins vs Aliens: S1 ~ "Prom
King" (13 Screenplay-Novellas)
*40K ~ Survival University: Shorts &
Novelettes (Screenplays & Prose)
*35K ~ Young & Powerful Prequel:
Virgins, Vixens & Murder (Audioplay)
*35K ~ Sex, Truth & Videotape: Shorts &
Novelettes (Plays & Prose)
*30K ~ Princess Wars: Sleeping Beauty
& Curse of Pirate Isle (Prose)
*30K ~ Dear Recruiter: Spykult Shorts &
Novelettes (All Prose)
*30K ~ The Diary of Christi Luv: Poetry
& Song ~ Life Songs (Rhyme)
*30K ~ The Diary of Christi Luv: Poetry
& Song ~ Love Songs (Rhyme)
*25K ~ Love Me Tender: The Existence
of Sound (Screenplay)
*20K ~ Literary Rants of A 13 Yr. Old Kid:
Shorts & Flash-Fiction (Prose)

NOVELETTES & SHORT-FILM POC PLAYS (7K - 17K WORDS & PRESUMABLY 30 TO 60 MINUTES IN ADAPTED SCREEN TIME):

*15K ~ Dear Recruiter: My CRAZY Big
Brother! (Prose)
*10K ~ Dear Recruiter: The
Superhero-Rape Experiment (Prose)
*10K ~ Dear Recruiter: TDOCL ~ My 1st
BF Was A Sociopath (Prose)
*10K ~ Survival University: 3 Shorts

(Stage & Screenplays)
*10K ~ Survival University: Angel DeVille
(Screenplay)
*10K ~ Survival University:
TDoCL/iBreathe Therefore iWrite
(Prose)
*10K ~ Survival University: KiLL Club
(Prose)
*10K ~ Survival University: Jack In The
Box (Screenplay)
*10K ~ Sex, Truth & Videotape: TDoCL ~
There's That Hair! (Prose)
*10K ~ Sex, Truth & Videotape: Dr.
Apocalypse! (Screenplay)
*10K ~ Sex, Truth & Videotape: Will
Power (Screenplay)
*10K ~ Sex, Truth & Videotape: The
Rumor Mill (Screenplay)
*10K ~ Sex, Truth & Videotape: Hottie
Wars ~ Cyborg Adventure (Play)
*10K ~ Literary Rants of A 13 Yr old Kid:
Unfinished Business (Prose)
*10K ~ Philosophies Explained: Logic of
Luv's Cursed Books (Mix)
*10K ~ Philosophies Explained: Logic of
Luv's Trapped Books (Mix)
*10K ~ Philosophies Explained: Logic of
Luv's Puzzled Books (Mix)
*10K ~ Philosophies Explained: Logic of
Luv's Invaded Books (Mix)
*10K ~ Philosophies Explained: Logic of
Luv's Awakened Books (Mx)
*10K ~ The Diary of Christi Luv:
Poetry&Song/Political Life (Rhyme)
*10K ~ The Diary of Christi Luv:
Poetry&Song/Faith Life (Rhyme)
*10K ~ The Diary of Christi Luv:
Poetry&Song/Youth Life (Rhyme)
*10K ~ The Diary of Christi Luv:
Poetry&Song/Puppy Love (Rhyme)

*10K ~ The Diary of Christi Luv:
Poetry&Song/Bad Love (Rhyme)
*10K ~ The Diary of Christi Luv:
Poetry&Song/ForeverLove (Rhyme)

SHORT STORIES & SKIT-LENGTH POC PLAYS (1K - 7K WORDS & PRESUMABLY 5 TO 30 MINUTES IN ADAPTED SCREEN TIME):

***5K ~ 3 Shorts: The Hunt Brothers
(Screenplay)
***5K ~ 3 Shorts: The Soul Savers
(Screenplay)
***5K ~ 3 Shorts: The Happy Hope
Heroes (Stageplay)
***5K ~ Literary Rants of A 13 Yr Kid: 1
Last Kiss For The Runaway Boy
***5K ~ Literary Rants of A 13 Yr old Kid:
Cyclone's House

FLASH FICTION & AD-LENGTH POC PLAYS (UNDER 1K WRDS & PRESUMABLY UNDER 5 MINUTES IN ADAPTED SCREEN TIME):

*TBA ~ Literary Rants of A 13 Year-old
Kid: Various Unlisted Segments

IN PROGRESS...

*TBA ~ Breathe. (Novel)
*TBA ~ Superhero Wars: The Crossover
Games (Novel)
*TBA ~ Zombie Wars: *NSYNC SAVES
THE WORLD! (Screenplay)
*TBA ~ Pop Star Wars: NSYNC vs BSB ~
Boy Band Battle (Screenplay)
*TBA ~ Supervillains In Love: The
Musical (Screenplay)

AD-LENGTH = Quick TV Commercial Length

<u>*SKIT-LENGTH* = *Long Sneak Preview Length*</u>
<u>*POC* = *Proof of Concept*</u>
~

<u>~ *ORDER OF BOOKS BY YEAR OF COPYRIGHT* ~</u>
<u>Most concepts/titles are not listed because they are not yet in development.</u>
Entire Title May Not Be Spelled Out But Represents Series Franchise
~ 1990's ~
<u>1990's COPYRIGHT OF COMPLETED SHORT & FULL LENGTH SCRIPTS</u>
MOST NEW CONCEPTS/TITLES: Original = 1997-2002 / 1st Published = 2017
LITERARY RANTS/13YRKID: 1st Scripts = 1997 / 1st Published/Proofed = 2020
***********HUNTING LOVE: Idea/Title = 1997 / 1st Published/Updated = 2017
************WILL POWER: Idea/Title = 1998 / 1st Published/Updated = 2020
***POEM/SONG~SAMPLER: Original = 1999 / 1st Published/Updated = 2019
POEM/SONG~COLLECTION: Original = 1999 / 1st Published/Updated = 2020
*POEM/SONG~YOUTH LIFE: Original = 1999 / 1st Published/Updated = 2020
**POEM/SONG~FAITH LIFE: Original = 1999 / 1st Published/Updated = 2020
POEM/SONG~POLITIC LIFE: Original = 1999 / 1st Published/Updated = 2020
**POEM/SONG~BAD LOVE: Original = 1999 / 1st Published/Updated = 2020
POEM/SONG~PUPPY LOVE: Original = 1999 / 1st Published/Updated = 2020
POEM/SONG~FOREVER <3: Original = 1999 / 1st Published/Updated = 2020
*POEM/SONG~LIFE SONGS: Original = 1999 / 1st Published/Updated = 2020
POEM/SONG~LOVE SONGS: Original = 1999 / 1st Published/Updated = 2020
~ 2000's ~

<u>2000's COPYRIGHT OF COMPLETED</u>
<u>SHORT & FULL LENGTH SCRIPTS</u>
MANY NEW CONCEPTS/TITLES:
Original = 2002-2010 / 1st Published =
2020
PROM KING (Virgins vs Aliens basis):
Movie Script = 2000 / 1st Pub = 2020
BITE ME: My Valley-Girl-Wolf Idea =
2005 / TP's Valley-Boy Spin/Play = 2008
************JACK IN THE BOX: 1st Script =
2005 / 1st Published = 2020
ALIEN WARS/PERFECT CHILD:
Idea/Title = 2005 / 1st Published = 2017
*****COMET/LADY PHANTOM:
Idea/Title = 2007 / 1st Published = 2017
****************ANGEL WARS: 1st Script =
2008 / 1st Published = 2017
**TP'S THE BOY NEXT DOOR: 1st Script
= 2009 / 1st Published = 2020
~ 2010's ~
<u>2010's COPYRIGHT OF COMPLETED</u>
<u>SHORT & FULL LENGTH SCRIPTS</u>
SOME NEW CONCEPTS/TITLES:
Original = 2013-2017 / 1st Published =
2017
*****PROPHET WARS: Concept/Title =
2010 / 1st Published/Updated = 2020
*****PRINCESS WARS: Concept/Title =
2010 / 1st Published/Updated = 2017
*********SIREN WARS: Concept/Title =
2010 / 1st Published/Updated = 2017
**************ANGEL DEVILLE: 1st Script =
2013 / 1st Published = 2020
********THE HUNT BROTHERS: 1st Script
= 2013 / 1st Published = 2020
***********THE SOUL SAVERS: 1st Script =
2013 / 1st Published = 2020
********HAPPY HOPE HEROES: 1st Script
= 2013 / 1st Published = 2020
************THE RUMOR MILL: 1st Script =

2013 / 1st Published = 2020
*******************KiLL CLUB: 1st Script =
2013 / 1st Published = 2020
*********YOUNG & POWERFUL: 1st Script
= 2013 / 1st Published = 2020
************LOVE ME TENDER: 1st Script =
2015 / 1st Published = 2020
ALIEN WARS/PERFECT CHILD: 1st
Script = 2015 / 1st Published = 2017
*SECRETS OF SKYLER STONE: 1st
Script = 2015 / 1st Published = 2017
*************PROPHET WARS: 1st Script =
2015 / 1st Published = 2020
****************SIREN WARS: 1st Script =
2017 / 1st Published = 2017
****************ANGEL WARS: Updated =
2017 / 1st Published = 2017
*************PRINCESS WARS: 1st Script =
2017 / 1st Published = 2017
**************HOTTIE WARS: 1st Script =
2017 / 1st Published = 2017
**********TP's IN HIS SHOES: 1st Script =
2017 / 1st Published = 2020
VIRGINS vs ALIENS (Prom King Update):
New Scripts = 2018 / 1st Pub= 2020
*****************THE PARTY: 1st Script =
2018 / 1st Published = 2019
*SHADOW WARS/GIN STORY: 1st Script
= 2019 / 1st Published = 2020
**DEAR RECRUITER: 1st Poem/Idea/Title
= 2019 / 1st Published = 2020
~ 2020's ~
<u>2020's COPYRIGHT OF COMPLETED
SHORT & FULL LENGTH SCRIPTS</u>
*A FEW NEW CONCEPT/TITLES:
Original = 2017-Now / 1st Published =
2020
*******************WILL POWER: 1st Script =
2020 / 1st Published = 2020
HAPPY ANVRSY DR APOCALYPSE: 1st

Script = 2020 / 1st Published = 2020
**MY 1ST BF WAS A SOCIOPATH: 1st
Script = 2020 / 1st Published = 2020
**iBREATHE THEREFORE iWRITE: 1st
Script = 2020 / 1st Published = 2020
*******MY CRAZY BIG BROTHER: 1st
Script = 2020 / 1st Published = 2020
SUPERHERO-RAPE EXPERIMENT: 1st
Script = 2020 / 1st Published = 2020
*********SURVIVAL UNIVERSITY: 1st
Series = 2020 / 1st Published = 2020
*****SEX, TRUTH & VIDEOTAPE: 1st
Series = 2020 / 1st Published = 2020

<u>COPYRIGHT OF CONCEPTS & TITLES
NOW IN DEVELOPMENT</u>
***SUPERHERO WARS: Concept/Title =
2010 / 1st Published Script = 2020
******MONSTER WARS: Concept/Title =
2010 / 1st Published Script = 2020
*******ZOMBIE WARS: Concept/Title =
2010 / 1st Published Script = 2020
***********BREATHE.: Concept/Title = 2010
/ 1st Published Script = 2020
***LUV HI5IQ GUIDES: Concept/Title =
2015 / 1st Published Script = 2020
***LUV HOW 2 WRITE: Concept/Title =
2015 / 1st Published Script = 2020
*HERO IS NEW BLACK: Concept/Title =
2015 / 1st Published Script = 2020
PROTECT OUR YOUTH: Concept/Title =
2015 / 1st Published Script = 2020
*****POP STAR WARS: Concept/Title =
2018 / 1st Published Script = 2020
****ROCK STAR WARS: Concept/Title =
2018 / 1st Published Script = 2020
*******NSYNC VS BSB: Concept/Title =
2018 / 1st Published Script = 2020
*TP'S LOVE MUSICALS: Concept/Title =
2018 / 1st Published Script = 2020
**LUV MEGA SAMPLES: Concept/Title =

2018 / 1st Published Script = 2020
*LUV GENRE SAMPLES: Concept/Title =
2018 / 1st Published Script = 2020
SUPERVILLAINSinLOVE: Concept/Title
= 2019 / 1st Published Script = 2020
*****KIDS WHO RAPED KIDS:
Concept/Title = 2020 / 1st Published
Script = 2020
PHILOSOPHY EXPLAIN: Concept/Title =
2020 / 1st Published Script = 2020
WHAT ACTOR R YOU?: Concept/Title =
2020 / 1st Published Script = 2020
NSYNC SAVES WORLD: Concept/Title =
2020 / 1st Published Script = 2020

**_List will be updated over time as more
titles/scripts are completed!_**

Only the guilty will be held accountable for their crimes.

<u>No innocent and/or undeserving people will ever be harmed, ended, or otherwise hurt because of something I wrote, typed, published or said.</u>

<u>I Affirm</u>
<u>This Belief Now:</u>

No one can use my creative works or media consumership-- or anyone's else's-- to inflict harm on an innocent person or pet. The practice of using the media to harm innocents is now over.

No one will allow any harm or health concern to come to my actual legitimate non-impersonated non-clone mother, Trudy Perkins, who raised me as a child. I see now that the reason why the version of her who lives with me can't sing like her is that she's the clone of my mom, whereas my real mom can sing circles around her clone-- because she knows how to use her vocal instrument. I just don't know where my real mom is. My mother's clone will be admitted to a mental hospital-- unharmed. Give them both perfect health now. I will update my published books accordingly...

And all of my & my pets' bioterrorists are now floating indefinitely

in outer space...

...as I and the ones I love who love me back all enjoy my $999 Billion Dollars in reparations-- with which

wonderful beautiful
things will happen.